BBQ BLUEPRINT

BBQ BLUEPRINT

TOP TRICKS, RECIPES, AND SECRET INGREDIENTS
TO HELP MAKE YOU **CHAMPION OF THE GRILL**

BILL WEST

BBQ
Blueprint

Essential Tricks, Tips, Recipes & Secret Ingredients
to Make You Champion of the Grill

Bill West

First Edition

Copyright © 2016 by Triehouse Publishing

All rights reserved. This book was self-published by the author Bill West under Triehouse Publishing. No part of this book may be reproduced in any form by any means without the express permission of the author. This includes reprints, excerpts, photocopying, recording, or any future means of reproducing text. If you would like to do any of the above, please seek permission first by contacting us at http://barbecuetricks.com

ISBN-13: 9781533425966
ISBN-10: 1533425965

Thank You and a FREE Book

Thanks for checking out BBQ Blueprint. If you like what you see, you'll love my first book "BBQ Sides and Sauces." It's loaded with more photos and recipes from the pages of BarbecueTricks.com.
I want to give it to you for free just to say thanks for reading.

To Download, go to
www.barbecuetricks.com/free-newsletter/

TABLE OF CONTENTS

ABOUT THE AUTHOR

INTRODUCTION

1. BBQ DEFINED 1
2. TOOLS OF THE TRADE 33
3. FUEL THE FLAME 51
4. METHODS AND MEATS 65
5. FIVE MAJOR BBQ FOOD GROUPS 91
6. FINISHING TOUCHES (SAUCES) 129
7. SECRET INGREDIENTS
   AND PANTRY ESSENTIALS 163
8. DIFFICULT DESSERTS 169
9. TOP TIPS AND SOME WARNINGS 187

ABOUT THE AUTHOR

Barbecue is a state of mind. A low and slow, feel good, process that should be savored. That's what Barbecue Tricks – the site at **BarbecueTricks.com** and the YouTube channel – want to encourage.

The site was started by Country Radio DJ, Bill West, to help share some useful foodie tips he was collecting hanging around South Carolina's best Pit Masters. West is on air host and Operations Manager of Charleston's leading radio stations and has interviewed some of entertainment's biggest celebrities including Taylor Swift, Darius Rucker, Paula Deen, Zac Brown, Ryan Seacrest, Garth Brooks, Keith Urban, Carrie Underwood and Alton Brown.

The tips and tricks caught on because they simply helped backyarders with grilling and BBQ problems. His online video channel has accumulated over 23,000 subscribers and more than 3 million video views. In 2010, he launched a weekly video podcast called GRATETV along with Pit Master friend, Jack Waiboer, and really started to build a tribe of fans. Says West, "The show is always a beer in length and is all about BBQ, recipes, learning, and having a low and slow good time."

West served as one of the founding board members for the Southern Barbecue Network and is a certified SBN judge.

West lives in Mount Pleasant, SC with his wife MJ, and teenage, guitar slinging son, Jack.

BILL WEST

INTRODUCTION

It's NOT about winning or losing. It's about low & slow. Or maybe that's just me.

But it seems there are three types of Barbecue people... Here's my breakdown:

1. Competition / Fighters
2. Backyarders
3. Eaters Foodie Fans

I made this book for all three to love.

Have you always wanted to bring home the blue ribbon in your local BBQ cook-off?

Or maybe you're just curious to hear what the best pit masters in America do to create succulent feasts for the masses!

A lot of pit masters are competition freaks. Super serious about every last dash of paprika. Some are really good at bluster, bragging, and blowviating about their outcome. Less in it for the culinary and more about the fight. Highly competitive. It's become the spectacle you see on cooking competition shows. Perhaps another trophy will get them closer to the promised land. Some have true fun with the competitions.

Then there's the Backyarder. They see the competition and are more of the DIY type. BBQ is the good ol' boy's culinary track. It's fun to see if you can make it right in the backyard. Surprise, even when it comes out "wrong" it still gets rave reviews and tastes pretty darn good.

Lastly, there are the Eaters. Probably the silent majority. Simply put - this crew loves to eat. BBQ is a worthy object of affection. Lots of variety. There's a unique culture of camaraderie, and there's usually an element of family memories, nostalgia, or traditions that takes the fandom to higher levels of fanaticism.

As for me, I never liked bragging or chest thumping. I'm the silent griller. Iv'e discovered I fall between Backyarder and eater but have learned a lot about the competition world in my studies. In fact...I discovered that there is a secret place in the COMPETITION world for guys like me and a lot of eaters and backyarders out there. I'll tell you about that in the coming pages. Plus competition curious cookers can pick up a few secrets I've learned along the way from pro Pit Masters like Jack Waiboer, three time South Carolina state champion. He's a guy that for years has literally taught the class on competition barbecue.

I would classify myself as a hybrid between the backyarder and BBQ foodie fan. I like to keep it simple and laid back but am serious and interested enough to seek out some really cool tricks to perfect whatever's roasting on the grill.

Plus some foodies may not want to go through all the hassles and expense of competitions, but love to eat that level of quality. The tricks are fun for all.

In this book, we'll help you to hone your barbecue fundamentals, master the grill and discover secret recipes you'll return to for a lifetime.

The recipes here range from essentials to just fun. You'd never do Beer can Chicken in a competition but every "meat head" needs to have the trick in his or her arsenal. In these pages are years of shortcuts and secrets that can cut weeks of wasted time off your culinary grilling exploration. It's been fun learning these tricks, but it's more fun not having to learn the hard way. Especially the thing about having a fire extinguisher handy and that other thing about NOT using scented garbage bags.

Forgive us in advance if a few of the revelations seem obvious. Somewhere down the line, the point wasn't obvious to someone.

So is this the book you're looking for? The following pages will be an easy read and assist not only the seasoned Competitor but the Backyarder and Eaters will enjoy more than a few short cuts that have been discovered through years of patient practice.

USA Bbq

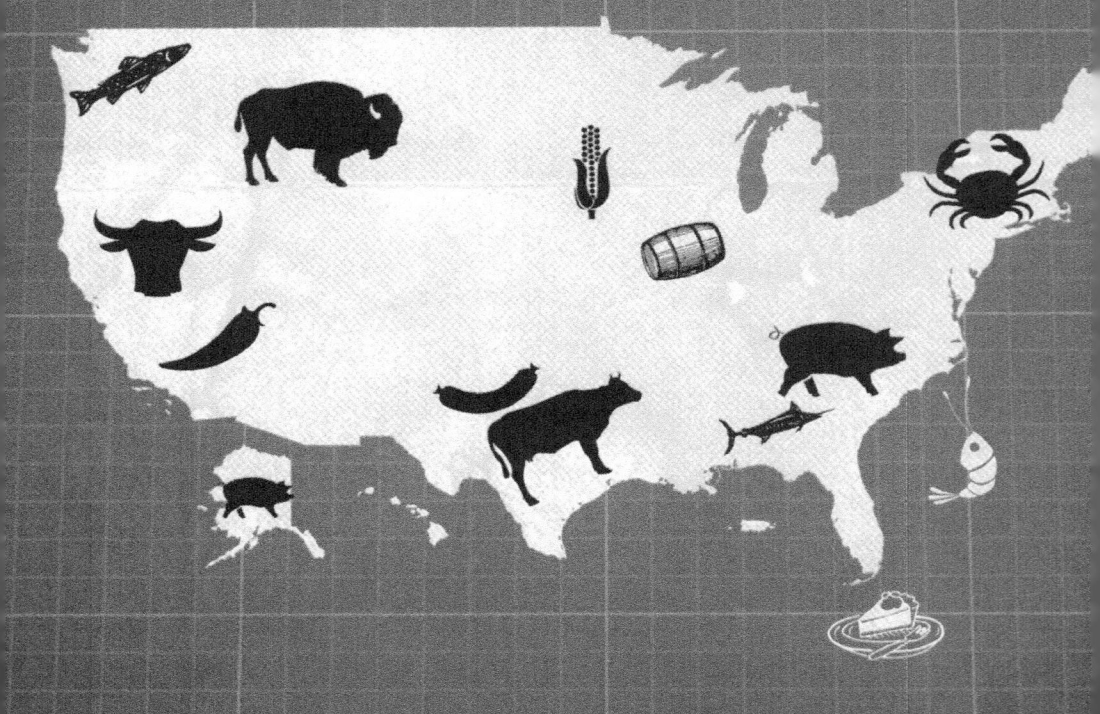

Chapter 1
BBQ DEFINED

" Southern barbecue is the closest we have in the US to Europe's wine or cheeses. Drive 100 miles and the barbecue changes. "

— **John Shelton Reed**

Chapter 1

To compete or just eat? Everyone has a different perspective on the BBQ life. These days the competition Good ol' Boys are all over TV trash talkin' anyone with a cleaver and apron. Somehow that never appealed to me. Just seems that a few guys take things way too seriously in the name of competition.

The BBQ world is on the brink of an explosion in popularity. In fact a lot of people and families have never even attended a pro cook-off or competition – let alone entertained the thought of cooking in one.

The great thing is that for a lot of people in America and the world, BBQ is about recreation...taking it low and slow.

Still there are a lot of different opinions on what BBQ is. Hang out with Kansas City BBQ Society cookers and they'll have you thinking the only thing people want is pulled pork, ribs, and chicken. But according to a recent survey by Weber, the three foods most often grilled are hamburgers (73 percent), chicken (41 percent) and steak (40 percent). Being from Chicago originally, my roots are more in hotdogs than whole hogs (but I love both).

In fact about 70 percent of Americans (21 and older) own a smoker or a grill and three fourths of the grill owners say they fire up the grill at least once a week during the grilling months (and those numbers are increasing).

It's complicated. No one agrees on how to spell BBQ, barbeque, barbecue, Bar-B-Que, etc. The word is used as a verb and a noun. Purists insist it's always a low and slow process, but most hot and fast grillers over a charcoal kettle consider themselves working the barbecue too. Heck, these days "barbecue" is a FLAVOR of pizza and potato chips.

BARBECUE IN THE HISTORY BOOKS

Many scholars will look back and attribute barbecue as a word derived from the term BARBACOA. They say Christopher Columbus noted Spanish settlers who cooked in a style featuring a grid of green sticks over indirect campfire heat they deemed barbacoa.

According to some at the South Carolina group DiscoverSouthCarolina.com, it was near Santa Elena or modern day Parris Island that the Spanish and American Indians forged BBQ history around a flickering campfire. Pit Master and Whole Hog Historian Jack Waiboer spelled it out for me, "The Spanish had pigs, and the Indians had developed unique cooking techniques." It's in these pits where the magic occurred – where swine turned to succulence. Everything was up on a grate. The Indians were cooking that way already when the hog came to America, and that's how pit cooked barbecue came about...It was the pig meeting the sacred fire pit. And thankfully for each and every one of us, it occurred on South Carolina shores." The South Carolina Department of Tourism goes even more in depth at SCBBQTrail.com.

ALL AMERICAN BBQ?

Is barbecue an American phenomenon? Sort of. It's true that America loves its barbecue - remember the old cheery Chevy slogan "Baseball, Hotdogs Apple Pie and Chevrolet"? It leads to perhaps grilling hotdogs, but the picture doesn't end there. Sure, internationally there is "Shrimp on the Barbie" in Australia (was that a thing or just a steakhouse commercial?) Jamaica definitely has unparalleled Caribbean jerk flavors of charred chicken, scotch bonnets, and allspice...There's Chinese, Mongolian BBQ,

Brazilian steakhouses and more; still, barbecue in the Americas seems very homegrown. In fact, some say that it seems there's a different specialty for every nook or region in the US.

"Southern barbecue is the closest we have in the US to Europe's wine or cheeses. Drive 100 miles and the barbecue changes." - John Shelton Reed

Let's take a road trip:

In the Pacific Northwest you could say salmon is a cedar plank barbecue specialty; down in California the Santa Maria tri-tip is all the rage, but further in the south the story changes to low and slow wood fired bark coated glorious slabs of pork; and in Texas, it's beef. A detour in Alabama will find a peculiar chicken with a unique sideshow of white sauce. Kansas City and Memphis are all about the ribs. At the Kentucky Derby, you might find a three-meat burgoo (stew) with venison or pork, rabbit or chicken, mutton, vegetables and black sauce. If you're looking for goat, check parts of Texas and Mississippi. Sausage is legendary in central Texas too. Finally, you can really go whole hog in the Carolinas. Not only with select pit masters like Rodney Scott of Scott's barbecue in Hemingway, South Carolina serving up incredibly succulent hardwood smoked whole hog, but also the Carolinas are home to the widest array of sauces AND and one of the only places to find HASH.

North Carolina and South Carolina are an odd pair. Yankees almost see the duo as the same State - "Carolina." But there are differences; especially when it comes to barbecue sauce. It's somewhat regional, but everyone has his or her own favorite. Up Northeast, they like a close to pure vinegar version of an ultra thin sauce. I've even seen it clear (although usually using cider vinegar).

South Carolina has it's hands in different styles, but their claim to fame (thanks to Maurice Bessinger and family) is a tangy sweet mustard based sauce. In the Piedmont area, or out West, it's also vinegar. But there's a good squirt of tomato or ketchup in the mix. We'll cover all of them here... but first -

The Palmetto state is home to a different kind of Barbecue sauce. Its Northern brethren in Western North Carolina have staked their claim in a vinegary thin and spicy sauce that cuts the fattiness of whole hog pulled pork. But South Carolinians like to keep their options open, and SC is, in fact, one of the only places you can find a different – mustard based style of barbecue sauce.

The origins of the mustard infusion is said to have been passed down from German influences from settlers on the Carolina coast. In the mid 1700s, the British Colony of South Carolina brought in thousands of families to the area to settle in and make the state their home. They brought with them traditional German fare with the common use of mustard. To this day, most of the biggest names in South Carolina are of German decent including the Bessinger family who still wave the mustard flag in their BBQ joints in the Columbia and Charleston area.

The thought of a mustard sauce is foreign to many fans, tend to like this tangy take on a thick sweet sauce. There are hundreds of variations that can be created with different varieties of mustard but tradition leads to a simple, affordable yellow blend that we've adapted below. This mainstream blend of mustard and vinegar makes for another tangy way to cut through fatty pulled pork at your next pig pickin'.

Deep in the heart of Texas the BBQ pride courses through the veins of the pit masters as if their blood was mop sauce! Texas BBQ is uniquely Beef. Fresh sausage (like the zesty Jalapeno sausages from Kreutz Market) come in as a popular second favorite. Mesquite is a popular wood across the state, but Post Oak is the popular choice for particular smokers like Aaron Franklin of Franklin BBQ in Austin and my favorite, Lockhart BBQ near Dallas.

The sauce in Texas, – if the joint allows (Kreutz doesn't) - is more of a tomato based tangy variety. Also, it is occasionally served heated like in Eddie Deen's, near Cowboy's Stadium.

In California, the Santa Maria styled tri-tip is defining protein in smokers. The pit masters of the Santa Maria Valley in Central California focus on the triangular shaped roast from the lower area of the sirloin. Unlike brisket, this beef is best served medium rare with a unique dry rub. Also served with pinquito beans and salsa. Wood fired over a live fire of red oak using a unique and very cool grill grate that can be raised and lowered to adjust heat over the fire.

Kentucky has bourbon sauces of course but is also the home of an unusual black sauce that is unique for lamb and mutton. Mutton has become a Western Kentucky thing.

Alabama adds a unique white sauce to the mix.

Georgia's contribution is boiled peanuts and Brunswick Stew. Brunswick Stew is kind of like a Burgoo or "Hash" in Carolina (different, though, as hash is served over rice in the Carolinas.)

Memphis is renowned for the quintessential BBQ competition "Memphis In May" and dry rub ribs that have been perfected at downtown's legendary Rendezvous, my wife's favorite.

According to Eater.com, Kansas City boasts the most BBQ restaurants per capita than any other metro area in the U.S. They also have the obvious privilege to brag about being the home of KCBS "The Kansas City BBQ Society." The most prominent of the competition sanctioning groups. They are at the center of the thick sweet molasses sauce universe, thanks to KC Masterpiece commercial BBQ sauce that was founded there in 1977 by the late entrepreneur and psychiatrist, Richard Davis (who died in 2015). He sold the sauce to Kingsford in 1986.

Regional Beverages also seem to go hand in hand with BBQ. Cheer wine, RC Cola, Sun Drop, Red Rock, Big Red (Texas) and Sweet Tea are just a few area favorites.

TO COMPETE OR JUST EAT ?

So where do you fit in? Do you have what it takes to be one of the competition BBQ fanatics? Know that the competition routine is a lot of work but can be super rewarding. If you win a lot, it can be financially rewarding too. However, you may want to consider a different angle to get involved in the competition world.

After trying my hand in some KCBS and independent competitions I came to the conclusion that for me, there were too many conflicts:

- Competition is expensive
- Competing more than occasionally is too time consuming for someone with a full work week
- I don't really cherish "roughing it" on limited sleep in camping conditions

On the other hand, I noticed the judges were in short supply and highly respected and appreciated. The judges seemed to be having a more relaxed time enjoying barbecue. They pulled in to the competition judges' tent bright eyed and chatty and well rested (while the cooks on site were bleary eyed with the scent of hickory and beer on the skin. Oh yeah, the judges were eating like kings and didn't have to wash a single dish either!

So the reality for me is that the real way to enjoy a BBQ competition is in the judging. Sanctioned BBQ groups promote extensive judges training prior to the competitions. The training is thorough but fun and comes at a reasonable cost. There is also the cost of membership in your sanctioning group, but the annual fees are usually very reasonable and also do a lot for charitable organizations. The time commitment for a typical competition is very manageable. Saturday morning at 8:00 AM until about 1:00 – 2:00 PM. Saturday contests are typical. Seriously, skip breakfast, though.

Consider this: Judging may also be an activity your spouse or significant other can sink their teeth into. I remember being pleasantly surprised when MJ showed enthusiasm and a "sign me up" attitude towards judging. You too may be surprised. See our list of respected groups below and get involved with some great people.

I'm sure there are a few BBQ fans that have no interest in the competition scene but want to cook BBQ at the same level of quality and consistency. Later in the BBQ Blueprint, we map out the basics on competition meats, techniques, and recipes. We will go in depth; but take note: competition recipes are geared towards making that first bite "pop" for a table of judges with a few preconceived notions.

The conflict I have trying to bridge the gap between the pit masters competition champion and recipes for the backyard cooker is that the final outcome has sensible differences.

In competition, the "turn in" box is also prepared to have a sheen. Lacquered bones win (my beloved Rendezvous dry would score low in visual appeal). Judges score against fall off the bone and deem them overcooked. Real people (like the ones eating in your backyard) rave over fall off the bone. Plus turn-in meats are meticulously trimmed of excess morsels of fat and extra skin (especially chicken). In the real world those are often my favorite bites, and yours too, I bet.

Finally, competition judges notoriously like SWEET. So everything leans that way. In addition, competition pit masters know their money relies heavily on that one and only bite. It must pop. So oftentimes the real recipes they use are a bit over enhanced with salt, flavor enhancers and sometimes nitrates to create a deeper smoke ring.

With brisket, it's about high end quality meat. Think expensive. Ironic since brisket traditionally was grown out of the resourcefulness in creating such a succulent treat out of what WAS a discounted, tough, and cheap cut.

So the basics behind competitions can get extreme. Use your own judgement on how close you need to get to pro level 'que.

JUDGING IS FREE FOOD & FUN

Perhaps you'll find you have a desire to be a certified judge. First off... some of the big BBQ sanctioning groups (KCBS and Memphis In May) have training classes you need to take so you may not be able to jump directly into the circuit day one, but it's not difficult. My first event was self sanctioned (they made up their own rules), and the group enlisted judges from a variety of other organizations. This is not uncommon and, in general, the attitudes around the judging tent seems to be fairly loose, laid back and ready to teach newbies. Don't be surprised if it seems a bit chaotic.

I learned that being a judge was, for me, better than competing.
Judging BBQ competitions may be right for you too if you are:

- Non competitive – I'm not selling a sauce, and a trophy isn't that big of a deal to me
- Hungry and love to eat – (yes, despite taking only a bite or two of each item you will leave very FULL)
- A foodie
- On a budget...I didn't want to spend the $$ on meat, charcoal, extras and an entry fee - It adds up
- Lacking free time – It takes two days to prep, cook, and compete while judging just takes a leisurely half-day Saturday

- Wanting to feel important - Teams lacking sleep will act silly when they see someone marked "judge"
- Fond of sleeping in a real bed with air conditioning
- Wanting to compete in the future

The last point is a good one. You get a whole new perspective on how serious (yes, one cooker missed his turn in time, and his chicken was eliminated) and sometimes subjective, judging can be. It is the best way to learn what the judges are looking for before you start competing.

A few things I learned from judging:

- Read the rules – you're only judged on what's listed.
- Appearance matters – it's usually an individual point in the judging. I saw a few boxes smudged with fingerprints (yuck) and sloppy with sauce. Layout the food in the box in a clean, orderly and attractive manner. In my case, they opened the box, and we all looked at it and simply judged "appearance" from 1 to 9. That was almost a third of the total potential score.
- Keep it hot. The pieces that were warmer seemed to taste better.
- Stay away from lighter fluid.
- Judges expect some sauce, in general like sweet, NOT heat.
- Perfect ribs won't fall off the bone (To a judge that's overdone), but they should bite off clean.
- Overall I was surprised how similar all the ribs were and how everything was still warm.

Judging is an economical way to experience the thrill of the grill without touching any charcoal and still getting a good night's sleep.

SANCTIONING ORGANIZATIONS

I did eventually get certified to judge by a sanctioned organization. If you are interested in getting started in the wild and wooly world of competition barbecue, check out the association nearest you. You may be shocked at the number of competitions in your state during any given weekend. If you want to judge or compete, you are sure to find a friendly group of new friends in the list below.

Arizona Barbecue Association (ABA) www.azbbqa.com
California Barbecue Association (CBA) www.cbbqa.com
Florida Barbecue Association (FBA) www.flbbq.org
Greater Houston Barbecue Society (GHBBQS) www.angelfire.com/tx/ghbbqs
The Greater Omaha Barbecue Society (GOBS) www.gobs.org
International Barbecue Cookers Association (IBCA) www.ibcabbq.org
The Iowa Barbecue Society (IABBQ) www.iabbq.org
Kansas City Barbecue Society (KCBS) www.kcbs.us
Lone Star Barbecue Association (LSBA) www.lonestarbarbecue.com
Memphis Barbecue Network (MBN) www.mbnbbq.com
Memphis in May (MIM) www.memphisinmay.org
Mid-Atlantic Barbecue Society (MABBQA) www.mabbqa.com/index.html
Mosquito County (FL) BBQ Society (MCBBQ) www.mcbbq.com
National BBQ Association (NBBQA) www.nbbqa.org
National BBQ Festival www.nationalbbqfestival.com
North Carolina Barbecue Society www.ncbbqsociety.com
New England Barbecue Association (NEBA) www.nebs.org
Pacific Northwest Barbecue Association (PNWBA) www.pnwba.com
South Carolina BBQ Association (SCB) www.scbarbeque.com
Southern Barbecue Network (SBBQN) www.sbbqn.com
South Carolina BBQ Association (SCBA) www.scbarbeque.com/events.html
Texas Gulf Coast BBQ Cookers Association (TGCBCA) www.tgcbca.org
World Barbecue Association (WBA) www.wbqa.com
World Food Championships (WFC) www.worldfoodchampionships.com

BACKYARD BBQ

Backyard BBQ doesn't sound nearly as sexy as all the TV and national competitions, but it remains the defining cornerstone of barbecue. The roots of backyard 'cue start with our parent's parents on rural farms butchering and curing and smoking meat as a preservation method. Fast forward to more modern times, and backyard barbecue means recreation. In 2014 Weber revealed a survey that proved grilling equals positive emotions too, showing 64% of grill owners say grilling is relaxing after a stressful day, and almost half of the survey said grilling reminds them of positive memories about growing up and seeing their parents grill. For me, that memory is Sunday suppers at my grandparents' house burning hot dogs on a Weber kettle using way too much lighter fluid. In the backyard, BBQ is ruled by a handful of tools: charcoal, wood fire, gas, and smoke, plus a surprisingly focused menu of favorites. Most popular: hamburgers, hotdogs, and steak.

BURGER NATION

When it comes to the backyard, the good ol' hamburger is our go-to protein. Usually with cheese as only about seven percent of people prefer it "without." Burgers are simply a summertime staple in the USA. Everybody can handle 'em. Still – your cookout might just go a bit smoother when you are ready to take on the grill with these quick tips and tricks for America's favorite BBQ food:

1. Keep it Together...Make your patty out of good ground beef. 80/20 (80 percent lean) is typically recommended. If you can get it freshly, ground you will enjoy better texture. Use some egg and bread crumbs too. Not only will it add flavor and moisture but it will help the beef hold together. (I have been beaten up on the website for adding fillers – chime in on the flogging at barbecuetricks.com).

2. Chill Out. Pop the patty in the freezer or fridge for fifteen minutes before hitting the grill. The chill will also help them hold together.

3. The Dent. You can help keep the patty from balling up by starting with a little dent in the center of the burger. When the meat cooks, the dent will diminish, and you'll have a flatter patty.

4. Plan Ahead. Have all your supplies on hand. Think through it before you put the meat on the fire. A trip back to the kitchen could mean disaster if there is a flare-up while you are gone.

5. Keep It Tidy. Start with a clean grill. Fire it up as hot as you can and then brush it clean. Oil with towel. The grill bits left over from Labor Day's cookout are NOT flavor enhancers!

6. Check Your Lid. Lid up? Or down? The rule is: if the meat is thicker than your palm close the lid. If thinner, keep your eye on it.

7. Keep it simple. Don't over season. But DO add a secret ingredient to a few patties for fun and conversation.

8. Get Cheesy. Add the cheese at the very end. Survey says favorites are American and Cheddar.

9. Is It Done Yet? Go medium well. It's best to use a thermometer. Should read about 140°F in the middle of the thickest part of the meat.

10. Let It Rest. When you're done, let it rest. Cutting or biting too soon will allow the savory juices to drain out onto the plate. Plus the cheese is HOT, right?! Let it rest ten minutes. It's tough, but worth the wait.

RECIPE NEXT PAGE »

SPECIAL BURGER SAUCE

Everybody can recite the recipe of McDonald's Flagship burger the Big Mac.
"TwoAllB eefPattiesSpecialSauceLettuce CheesePicklesOnionsOnASesameSeedBun."
But what about that "special sauce" recipe?

I don't have any connections at the golden arches... but I did eat a BigMac today and then I jumped on the internet to find the closest knock off I could find.

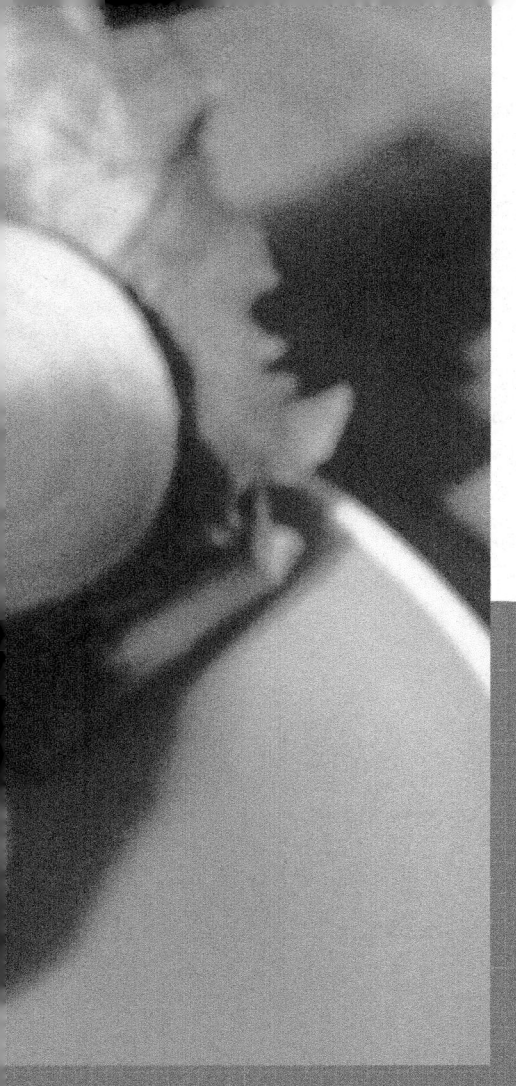

There are a bunch of options, but this one seemed the closest. After mixing up a dozen different BBQ sauces this week, this sauce stands out as something... well special. It was a real treat on a homemade burger.

But after 12.50 in ingredients maybe I should have just gone to McDonalds. Still, give this McDonalds Special Sauce Recipe knockoff a try. It rocks.

- ¼ cup real mayonnaise
- ¼ cup Miracle Whip
- 3 Tbsp creamy French salad dressing
- ½ Tbsp sweet pickle relish
- 1 ½ Tbsp dill pickle relish
- 1 tsp white sugar
- 1 tsp dried minced onion
- 1 tsp distilled white vinegar
- 1 tsp ketchup
- 1 dash salt

This Micky D's Knockoff nails the taste of the real thing. Even more "special" on a handmade burger patty. Combine all ingredients in a microwave safe bowl and mix. Microwave for 30 seconds. Mix again. Refrigerate until serving.

ALL AMERICAN HOT DOGS

Hot Dogs run a very close second in popularity to burgers, and honestly, they top my list for several reasons. They are cheap and readily available, easy to prepare (they're already cooked!) and hard to screw up. Even when you burn one, there is someone who likes it that way!

The national "Hot Dog and Sausage Counsel" (who knew there was even one of those?) say Americans typically consume about seven billion hotdogs over one summer. Just one summer! 155 million on the Fourth of July alone (is that you Joey Chestnut?). We love hotdogs because they're so easy. They are one of the best foods to freeze and keep in storage. When you find a great sale just freeze them nice & super compact in the corner of your freezer. They're good for six months - no problem

Some ground rules:

- Never eat a hotdog with utensils - got to use your hands
- It shouldn't take more than five bites to ever finish a hotdog
- Never offer wine at a hotdog cookout (just uncool)
- A hotdog should be considered a meal, not a snack
- For purists: No ketchup

First things first, and that's safety. One of the best things about hotdogs is that they are pre-cooked. Still you need to keep them cold until you cook them. It can get hot outside, and that's when bacteria like to grow, so keep them cold. Then never leave hotdogs at room temperature for longer than an hour or so. The general rule of thumb is never leave hotdogs or any outdoor food at room temperature for more than 2 hours and when you're talking about summer heat in the south - I would drop it down to one hour to be safe. Remember, I'm in the Lowcountry now, so it gets HOT!

Better yet, keep them hot. Once you do have them heated up on the grill, make sure you keep them up to temperature throughout the party - 140°F or hotter until you serve. Use an aluminum pan in the corner of the grill for a warming only zone.

Conversely, I usually also have a really hot zone.

YOU may not want a burnt hotdog, but there's one in every crowd that does. Bacon wrapping hot dogs is easy if you use one barbecue trick. Start with precooked thin sliced bacon to cut the flareups and just keep it secure after it softens up a little bit with a toothpick. Remember you don't have to actually cook the inside (hot dogs are precooked) so this way you don't have to worry about bacon grease flareups nearly as much.

Like burger beef, one trick to have a better tasting hot dog is starting with a higher quality hotdog (yep, usually the more expensive ones in the grocery store). Some of the best brands have been voted on, and the one that usually comes up the winner is Nathan's all beef with casing. It tops most of the "best of" lists, but it is a regional choice. As a native Chicagoan, I love Vienna All Beef hot dogs. Hard to find, though - especially in the south. The best trick is going with your local favorite.

Next - don't be a prick! In general, you don't want to "prick" or puncture your sausages. It lets the flavorful juice run out. This is not as big of a deal with hot dogs unless they are a super juicy variety. With Brats or sausages, you don't want to prick. However, when it comes to fun tricks for kids, I will advise you to try scoring the skin a few times. Try a spiral cut like we demonstrated on YOUTube or even get a gadget called the slot dog for giving a gator skin like affect to hot dogs for fun.

If you're doing a double dog - the trick to make them a little less awkward in a bun is to split each dog right down the center lengthwise. It will make the dogs less prone to slip around inside the bun.

Next, dress it up! Maybe that's a toasted bun (people love that) or just add toppings. A hot dog bar is a great idea so people can build their own perfect bite from sport peppers to relishes to cheese, yes even ketchup, anything goes. The one rule is keep it cool on ice so they won't go bad in the heat of the summer sun. Grab a muffin tin and keep it cold on a tray full ice.

Have fun with your toppings. There are also different styles of hotdogs. I love the Chicago style, and my favorite topping is actually celery salt. Seattle style hot dogs sound kind of cool too, with cream cheese on a toasted bun, grilled onions and sauerkraut. It's just a matter of favorites.

Always apply your condiments in order of wet first to dry last. Wet first, like mustard, chili, ketchup, then chunky next (relish, diced, onions cheese) and lastly the spices. Celery salt for me, thank you very much.

You can see why hot dogs are my favorite. So many options. Even with the bun (split top New England style?) You simply can't go wrong. Even a "bad" hot dog is still pretty good

DID YOU KNOW: Mustard predates the frankfurter by many a century. In ancient Roman times, it had many uses in medicine as well as in food. The Greeks used it to treat scorpion bites and just last summer my wife used it on a jellyfish sting.

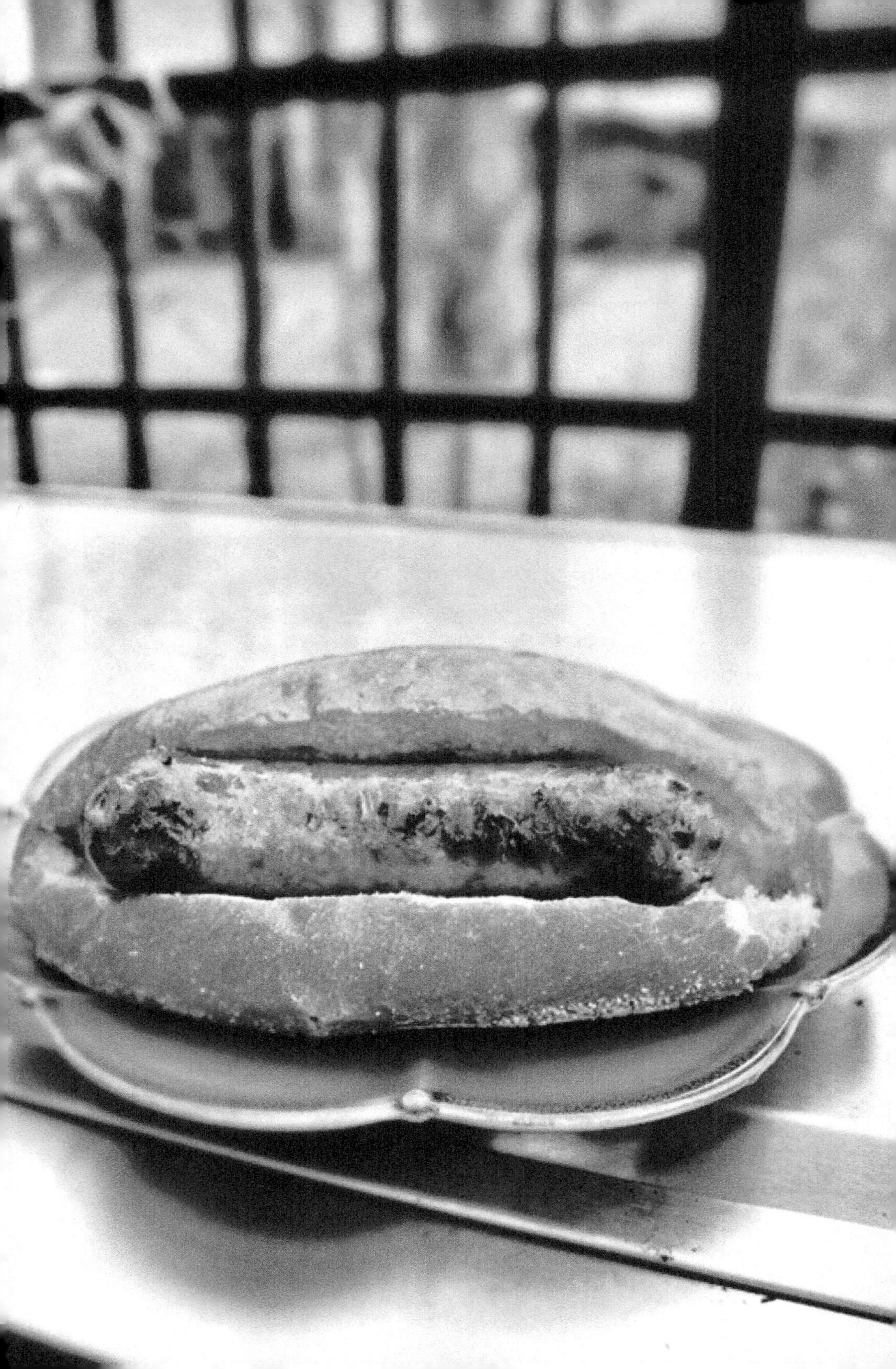

BRATWURST

Bratwurst are another tailgate and backyard favorite. Brats can be made out of beef, veal or pork. The ones most common here in the US are labeled all premium pork on the packaging. However bratwurst is an old German name. Derived from brät, which is finely chopped meat, and

Wurst, which means sausage.

Brats are almost like fine cheese in that there are so many different varieties. Forty different varieties if you want to go online and look them up.

They are fairly easy to cook, but the big thing you need to remember is that the inside of a brat (unlike a hot dog) is raw sausage. So you're gonna want to cook to the correct temperature like chicken or any other meat. The most basic way is going straight to the grill and for a lot of grillers that works just fine. You may want to brush it with a little light coating of oil before you hit the grill which can help add a little crisp texture to the casing. For best results, grill it over indirect heat for about 15-20 minutes. It's gonna take some time - usually longer than everything else on the grill, like burgers, so keep that in mind.

Indirect heat - which means not directly over the flames will allow you to get the internal temperature up a little slower and get the sausage hot enough without over-charring the rest of the brat. The other benefit is that it keeps the flare ups down.

You want the final product to appear golden brown with an unbroken skin if you can (don't worry too much about that it's hard to control).

Make sure you use an instant read thermometer to hit the recommended internal temperature of about 170°F if it's going to sit around a little bit longer. Remember just because the outside is charred the inside may not be done yet, so use a thermometer.

It's also common to pre-cook or par-boil the bratwurst in a pan from the comfort of the kitchen. Or use that side burner that you never use on the grill. Just add one or two inches of your favorite beer into a pan over medium heat. Add the sliced onions maybe some peppers and the brats.
Bring to the lowest possible simmer that you can. You don't want to boil it. You don't want to rupture the skin of the brats by getting the liquid too hot. Cook it for about 6 - 8 minutes and then you get to finish off on the grill like you did in the first procedure with a shorter grilling time only 3 - 6 minutes. That removes the worry about the inside being cooked.

The third way to cook brats is kind of a combination of the first two. It's been called a "Brat Tub", and I think it's the most fun way to cook brats. You will need a simple shallow pan with:

- butter
- onions
- green peppers
- a beer or two

Put the pan on the side of the grill over indirect heat, but get it hot.

This gives the brats a little hot bath after your first grilling step. That way, you can keep them cooking. You'll always have a hot brat on hand, you can pay attention to the game or socialize, and also eliminate some of the worry about internal temperatures from not cooking long enough. You don't have to hover over the grill as much.

A couple of other pointers:

Use tongs. Never a fork. You don't want to prick the casing. That would diminish the juiciness of the end product and would also encourage a big flare up.

And if you want to add a lick of smoke - even to a gas grill - you can toss in a foil smoker pouch full of wood chips under the grate before cooking.

STEAK:

"Big juicy steak" seems to go hand inand hand with living it up or treating yourself to something special. To most of us, a steak on the back yard grill is something special. But in fact, it's the third most popular meat to grill. However, it's still ("preferredtops" according to 62% of fans in Weber's recent survey) after Burgers (82%), hot dogs (75%). Steaks are also pricier. But how do you know what to buy?

"Steak" typically refers to a slice of meat or beef. Then there are the U.S. Department of Agriculture's (USDA) grades. The top three grades we can buy in stores are Prime, Choice, and Select. The grades are based on fat marbling and age (a good indicator of flavor). The grading is actually voluntary for the meat packer.

- Prime: Whatever the cut, there's more succulent marbled fat. This will make the Prime steak more tender and tastier than the other grades. Only the top few percent earn the prime label so you may not see them in a typical grocery store. Look to a butcher or gourmet grocer for that.
- Choice: This is what we most often get in the supermarket. Still a good choice for flavor and perhaps a better "choice" for your waistline (if you are watching fat levels.)
- Select: There is less fat marbling in the Select cut so it will be leaner and considered tougher. Again this is relative to the other grades of the same cut from the same packer.

COOKING THE PERFECT STEAK

All over, tailgate nation grillers will either overcook, undercook or serve up a steak that's as tough as a shoe! One trick is to get the grill super hot! It can't be hot enough to get that steak house char.

Season simply with sea salt and fresh black pepper.

Finally, when it's done, give it a rest! Never serve a steak hot off the grill; let it rest a minute or two on a warm platter.

There are hundreds of ways to cook a steak. Most BBQ aficionados and backyarders keep it simple. Fire up high heat and sear the beef and hope the middle is still good. The traditional thought is that the initial sear "Locks in juices." The reality is the sear will not lock in anything... it's kind of BS... in fact we've all seen a seared steak still pool with juices.

But the fast sear is fine for most – honestly, I could eat a steak no matter if you cooked it in a crock pot... even when it's bad – it's still pretty good....but lately, there has been talk of a reverse sear method. Here's the deal:

It's basically the opposite of that fast sear and bake. In this case you START the steak off low and slow – between 250 and 300 on indirect heat. You grill until the internal temperature reaches a temperature that is about ten degrees BELOW your final desired internal temp.

If you want it around 150 degrees - Medium (USDA may differ) target 140° with a quick read thermometer. Then pull it off the heat for a few minutes until it just starts to drop below 140°. That's your cue to fire up the high heat or searing burner and blast high heat on both sides to achieve the charred caramelization and crust. Pull off and enjoy.

Some experts say the low and slow reverse sear method gives you a more tender steak allowing natural enzymes some additional time to do some magic. Most say it wont affect flavor all that much – but I believe you do end up with a better char and crust.

LONDON BROIL

The term "London broil" does not refer to a specific cut of meat, but a method of preparation and cooking. Served rare to medium rare the cut of meat traditionally used is flank steak, but sometimes butchers will label top round steak/roast as London Broil.

It's typically a tougher cut. Here's tricks to get it tender:

One trick for tenderizing a tough cut is by using a meat mallet to break up tough fibers. You're almost pre-chewing it (Sorry that sounds gross). You are physically breaking up the fibers a bit; don't worry about the look just yet. In the end after you marinate, your BBQ will still look pristine. The thicker the cut, the more you can whack. Wrap the slab in plastic to avoid shirt staining splattering.

Next, use a nice marinade to soften the newly damaged fibers. Some grillers may choose to use a high acid marinade to boost the tenderizing effects. I use a simple mix of onion... light soy and liquid smoke... and let it marinate in the fridge for up to four hours.

So, in North America, London Broil is basically an affordable cut of beef - marinated - grilled and sliced thin. In Canada, London Broil is a ground meat patty wrapped in flank or round steak. Ironically, the dish is unknown in the English city of London, England.

Third, use the reverse sear method described earlier - cook it slow to an internal temp of about 120° -- then pull it off until the the center just starts to lower and finish the cook with a fast sear direct over red hot heat.

Allow the cooked meat to rest for 5 – 10 minutes or so before cutting AGAINST the grain of the meat fibers (or perpendicular to the strands of beef) in pencil thin slices.

EASY LONDON BROIL MARINADE

- **1 large 15oz. bottle of low sodium soy sauce**
- **Onion, sliced**
- **1 dash of liquid smoke**

GRILL MARKS

The signature sign of a great grill master is those perfect diamond or square grill marks. To keep your BBQ cred, they gotta look good on a steak or a piece of chicken or a chop. Here's how to do it:

- First, start with a clean grill. You don't want grime making the mark. You want it to be a true sear. With the grill clean, it's time to look at seasoning. Basically, with the seasoning, you don't want too much sugar. Sugar will simply burn on the surface of the meat. Use turbinado sugar when you must. It has a higher burn point.

- Place the meat on the grate and make sure it has good surface contact. Then, don't touch it for one fourth of the cooking time. Again don't touch for one quarter of the cooking time.

- After you've exercised your patience, give the meat a 45 to 90 degree rotation on the grill (remaining on the same side) for the rest (the second quarter) of the cooking time. Again, don't move it. You'll want to allow the sear to do its thing and actually release from the grill. If it is still sticking, you may need a bit more time.

- Once you think the whole piece is "half cooked" you can flip and check your results (repeat for the 2nd side. Inevitably one side will look better than the other. Present that side up on the plate.

This method also works well with indoor grill tops. Looks nice on veggies and even better on white meats.

CANADIAN STEAK SEASONING

Also known as "Montreal Steak Spice" or "Montreal" Steak Seasoning this coarse and distinct seasoning is made of coarse garlic, salt, and pepper and is considered the perfect compliment to beef. There is no sugar in this spice and that allows for a higher sear temperature as sugar burns too quickly. The recipe comes from a Montreal deli in the 1940's and 50s that originally used a similar combination of spices for smoked meat pickling spices. Although the exact recipe varies from steak house to steakhouse, here are the basics.

- **2 Tbsp black pepper from peppercorns (fresh ground is a must)**
- **1 Tbsp sweet paprika**
- **2 Tbsp coarse sea salt**
- **1 Tbsp dehydrated garlic**
- **1 Tbsp granulated onion**
- **1 Tbsp ground coriander**
- **1 Tbsp ground dill seed**
- **1 Tbsp red pepper flakes**

For best results bloom whole seeds, if available, in a pan over stove and grind whole seeds into a coarse rub. Store the mixture in an airtight container for up to a month.

MARINATED FLANK STEAK

Tenderizing can go a long way to boost the bite of an affordable cut of beef like a Flank steak. Use a heavy meat mallet to pound the tough fibers into broken submission and follow up with an acidic marinade to tenderize the fibers even more. Ready to try something a bit different for friends? We promise you'll look like the King of The Grill with this juicy marinated FLANK steak.

- **1 ½ pound beef flank steak**
- **¼ cup bourbon**
- **¼ cup Dijon mustard**
- **4 tsp Worcestershire sauce**
- **Dash salt and pepper**

Soak a 1 ½ pound flank steak for at least a few hours.

Sear the meat directly over your grill flames. Then move the steak away from the coals and roast to about 130°F for medium rare. You'll thank us later.

Chapter 2

TOOLS
of the Trade

> " I can't cook.
> I use the smoke alarm as a timer. "
> **– Carol Siskind**

Chapter 2

You're playing with fire. Literally. So first a word about fire safety. It would be irresponsible not to cover a few safety tips.

There is an exciting element of primal danger when working with live coals. Don't let it distract you! If you are working with somewhat unpredictable hardwood lump charcoal that crackles and pops, wear long pants and closed-toed shoes.

Here are the top five most useful fire safety tricks and tips:

1. Burnin' Down The House is a fun song to sing at the Cookout, but SAFETY FIRST! Don't grill in an enclosed area (indoors or the garage); use baking soda to control a grease fire, not water. Have a fire extinguisher (required if you plan to get into competitions), bucket of sand/salt, or garden hose on hand; and be sure your grill is on stable ground before firing it up.... And keep the grill away from anything remotely flammable. Even a wool or fire retardant blanket can be nice to have on hand to smother larger cuts of meat like a whole hog.

2. Don't do charcoal on a wooden deck. Whatever the fuel it's never a bad idea to use a fire resistant grill mat and stabilize the base of the grill on a flat surface. Start with the grill at least ten feet away from anything flammable. Vinyl siding may not catch fire, but it's been known to melt and warp next to a grill. Also, you never want to move a hot grill. Same deal with turkey frying.

3. If you're using GAS, always open the lid before lighting. If you have more than a few failed lighting attempts, stop and allow gas to

dissipate before re-trying to ignite. Eyebrows come in handy on a hot and sweaty day.

4. Gather all your ingredients first. You never want to leave the grill unattended. Dangerous flare-ups happen in seconds. Use long handled grill utensils.

5. The best way to check for proper doneness is with an instant-read meat thermometer -- ground beef needs to cook until 145°... Chicken is more sensitive to bacteria and needs to get to a minimum 165°.

COOKER 101

So many types of cookers... So little garage space! There's almost an infinite combination of cooker styles, types, and specialties. For the most part, they can first be categorized by fuels and then sorted by different shapes, sizes, and specialties.

Fuels include gas, charcoal, hard wood (logs), pellets, and even electric heat. More on fuels next chapter; but first, a look at the most popular shapes and sizes and what might be the best choice for you.

SHAPES AND SIZES

First off, bigger isn't necessarily better. When you look to buy a grill you first need to consider size. How much room do you have on your patio? Do you need a lot of cook/grill top space? If you only cook for two, you can spare yourself a lot of time, fuel, and purchasing dollars by staying small. But if you want to jump into large cuts of meat or competition you'll probably need something more.

Here are a few of the most popular vessels:

- Horizontal grills are one of the most popular styles of cooker especially when it comes to gas grills. They allow for multiple heat zones with ample space to spread out on the grill grate.

- Barrel Cookers are similar in layout to a horizontal grill. Barrel cookers are often – quite literally built from steel barrels, empty propane tanks, or drums. Fuel sources vary with barrel cookers but lean towards charcoal or wood. Traditional old time Pit masters typically utilize a fire box attached to the end of the barrel to stoke with wood logs. Thus providing a steady stream of hard wood smoke and indirect low heat. AKA a "stick burner."

- One special breed of cooker can be horizontal or vertical. The pellet cooker is a wood fired stove that is slowly (and accurately) stoked automatically to create a steady source of heat and hardwood smoke. The most popular brand is made by Traeger. Most of the brands operate the same. You purchase the fuel pellets (compressed hardwood that looks like hamster food) by the 20- pound sack. Fill the hopper and the auger slowly feeds the wood pellets into the small fire pot that can get incredibly hot. But you can control the heat with a thermostat. These cookers are cherished on the competition circuit because they still pass the "must cook with wood" rules that some sanction groups require. The "set it and forget it" convenience, and true wood smoke flavor you get is a dream come true. The downside: pellets can be proprietary and expensive. Check our resources at the website for the best prices and specials when we hear of them.

- Eggs. -The Big Green egg is the heavyweight champion of this category. And when I say heavy- I mean it (XXLs weigh almost 500 pounds). Ceramic cookers are known for their ability to get screaming hot and retain a steady and efficient heat. One drawback is that they come down in temperature very slowly, so you want to be cautious not to over shoot your target temperature. These ceramic cookers are known by many different brand names like Primo (made in the USA in Georgia) Kamado Joe, and others. No doubt backyarders LOVE their individual "egg" brands. The Big Green Egg marketing machine hosts EggFests all over the country for fans and even issue glossy magazines promoting the brand.

- Upright smokers. Upright smokers can look like small refrigerators, but they are a nice choice for easy smoking. Look for plug- in electric models that work off wood pucks.

- Kettles. - People seem to love kettles like Weber's -- because it's such a vivid reminder of their child hood. My grandfather was definitely a character. Not a gourmet by any stretch of the imagination - he made soup with ketchup, routinely burned steaks and served chopped spaghetti. But every Sunday, we would gather outside of the garage for hot dogs on the black kettle grill. I don't remember if it was a Weber (probably, as we were in Glenview, only a stone's throw from Weber's home town of Palatine, Illinois), but I can still taste the charcoal starter fluid.

- Bullet Smokers. -Sometimes called water smokers, "bullets" are similar to an upright smoker crossed with a kettle. Brinkmann makes a very affordable starter charcoal model that got me into the smoking world, but Weber has the more popular Smokey Mountain Cooker (in two sizes) that has a solid fan base with plenty of turn key recipes. The WSM, as it's called, is an excellent choice for competition cooking (you may need more than one) as a lot of the trial and error has been documented. They have won many competitions too.

- Pit BBQ. – One very traditional cooking method is in a pit. Pits are used both above ground and below ground. Above ground pits are utilized by some of the best BBQ restaurants in the South as pit masters can cook large amounts of large cuts of meat like whole hogs at Scott's Barbecue in Hemingway, SC. In these large rectangular grills, hard wood embers and coals are shoveled into the bottom of the pitt (at ground level) with the meat suspended indirectly on a grate two to three feet above. Below ground pits are used for traditional cooking like Hawaiian Luau pork.

- Roasting boxes. – One of the most interesting cookers I've used is the the La CajaChina. It is a simple plywood box lined with steel. Large enough for a small pig or several Boston butts – you top the box with a steel tray sized to hold a sack of lit charcoal. This "Cuban microwave" then roasts the meat inside from the top down like an oven. It's a super cool conversation piece at the cookout. But there are two drawbacks: No smoke flavor and clean up can be a pain.

- Tailgaters . –There are several good choices for portability. I recently discovered pie pan sized disposable grills made by Bic (the lighter company). If you are tailgating and looking for convenience, these five dollar "giant sterno" disks are worth a look.

DUTCH OVENS THE HEAVY EQUIPMENT:

Dutch oven cooking is on the fringe of the BBQ world but worth including in our overview. Lodge Cast Iron has been making cast iron since 1896 in South Pittsburg, Tennessee. The company is still family owned and is widely distributed across the U.S.

Lodge may corner the market on cookware but my "go to" Dutch oven guru is Gary House. Gary operates the popular Cooking Everything Outdoors blog at www.Cooking-Outdoors.com and has mastered the craft. He was kind enough to allow me to pass these pointers (in his own words):

6 CONCEPTS TO DUTCH OVEN TEMPERATURE CONTROL FROM GARY HOUSE

The key to successful outdoor Dutch oven cooking is knowing how many charcoal briquettes are required to produce a certain temperature inside of your Dutch oven while it is cooking.
The secret to this knowledge is understanding charcoal briquettes.

Types of charcoal
Charcoal briquettes produce more uniform heat than campfire coals or Lump charcoal, making your Dutch oven temperature easier to control. Brand-name briquettes have more consistent quality than bargain brands. They are consistent in size— about 2 inches square — which is important for predictable heat. Start with charcoal briquettes if you just beginning and experiment with live campfire coals as you progress.

How many briquettes do you need?
This is the basic foundation of Dutch oven cooking, once you know this, everything else falls into place. Take your Dutch oven's diameter in inches and double it.

- 8 inch Dutch oven = 16 briquettes
- 10 inch = 20 briquettes
- 12 inch = 24 briquettes
- And so on.

The total calculation is the number of standard-size charcoal briquettes you will need to heat your Dutch oven to approximately 325 degrees F for one hour. It is that simple.

Controlling temperature

Most Dutch oven beginners are familiar with cooking on a stove at home, cooking with bottom heat only and that can cause confusion when cooking outdoors with a Dutch oven.

Because heat rises, briquettes heat the bottom of a Dutch oven more quickly and directly than the top. The top rim of the lid draws the heat downwards, you will need to divide your briquettes between the top and bottom for even heating. Commonly referred to as the three up method and is effective on 8, 10 and 12-inch diameter Dutch ovens; larger size Dutch ovens may require more briquettes.

As an example:

- To heat an 8-inch Dutch oven to 325 degrees, you need 5 coals on the bottom and 11 coals on top. Sixteen coals total.
- To heat a 10-inch oven, you need 7 briquettes on the bottom and 13 on top. Twenty coals total.
- To heat a 12-incher, you need 9 briquettes on the bottom and 15 on top. Twenty-four coals total.

These guidelines will get you close enough that, with practice, you can understand exactly what works for your Dutch oven.

Briquette placement
Using the circle method of coal placement, place your bottom coals in a single circle aligned with the legs of your Dutch oven closer to the outside of the Dutch oven bottom, referencing the lip of the Dutch oven lid place your coals evenly around the perimeter.

If your recipe calls for temperatures higher or lower than 325 degrees, make adjustments by adding or subtracting 2 briquettes. Two briquettes equal approximately 25 degrees. Add these to the top of the Dutch oven, unless you need more heat on the bottom.

How long do briquettes last?
Today's charcoal briquettes last about 45 - 50 minutes. When recipes call for longer cooking times, start fresh replacement briquettes at 40 minutes. They will be ready to add to your Dutch oven when the original coals start losing their heat. Replace approximately 60% of the coals each 45 - 50 minutes of cook time.

Compensation for weather conditions will be required. On cold days, add a couple of more coals on the top and on a hot day remove a coal or two. Wind will play a significant roll in temperature control, it is best to shelter your Dutch oven from the wind with a windscreen if possible.
Following these basic concepts will insure your first adventures in Dutch oven cooking are a success. After practicing a few recipes, temperature control will become second nature, and you will no longer need to count as you become more proficient.

Here is one of my favorite beginner recipes, the same one I use in my Dutch oven classes.

BLACKBERRY COBBLER

For the cake mix:

- **1 stick butter**
- **2 cups flour**
- **2 cups sugar**
- **1 tbs baking powder**
- **1tsp salt**
- **1 ½ cups milk**
- **For the berries:**
- **4 cups fresh or frozen blackberries or 2 bags frozen (thawed)**
- **½ cup sugar**
- **1 ½ tsp fresh grated lemon zest**
- **¼ cup water**
- **1 tsp cinnamon**
- **10 or 12" Dutch oven (20 or 24 briquettes)**

Start your briquettes using the formula above to determine the quantity.

Rinse your fresh blackberries and drain, place them in a bowl with your sugar, lemon zest, water and cinnamon; mix well and set aside.

When your briquettes are ready, place the bottom circle of briquettes down and set your Dutch oven with the lid on top of the briquettes, then add the remaining briquettes to the lid to pre-heat your Dutch oven.

Now you can mix your cobbler batter. In separate bowl combine flour, sugar, baking powder, and salt; stir to mix. Add milk and beat until batter is smooth. Remove the Dutch oven lid, take one stick of butter and place in hot Dutch oven, stir until melted. Add your Blackberry mixture to the melted butter and pour your cobbler batter over the top

(A different variation of this would be to take your batter and pour that in first, and place your blackberries on top.)

Replace the lid and bake for 45 minutes.

Serve with vanilla Ice cream and enjoy!

Gary House's
6 GOLDEN RULES
for storing your
DUTCH OVEN

RULE #1

Never put away your Dutch oven dirty.

RULE #2

Never put away your Dutch oven wet.

RULE #3

Put a light coating of seasoning on your Dutch oven while it is warm from cleaning.

RULE #4

Air circulation prevents a rancid Dutch oven; store with the lid off or ajar.

RULE #5

Store your Dutch ovens in the house where the humidity is balanced.

RULE #6

Rotate your Dutch ovens when selecting one for a meal.
The one on the bottom in the corner that is all dusty is going bad on you!

MEAT THE DISCADA

A Discada is a wok-like cooker constructed out of an agricultural plow disk (or harrow disk). Sometimes called a cowboy wok the discada is also the name of a mixed meat Mexican dish for tacos (recipe below). John Haney of Alveron Cookers in South Carolina designed one for Jack Waiboer on an episode of GRATETV.

See the process here (it's one of my favorite episodes) at
http://youtu.be/vMtQUZejHHM

DISCADAS TACOS

Also known as "Tacos Al Pastor" this mixed meat Mexican delicacy is a street food favorite. The discada gets its name from a plow "disk" that has been converted into an outdoor wok over live fire. Although the exact recipe varies from what you may have on hand, here are the basics:

- ½ lb bacon, diced
- 4 cloves garlic, minced
- 8 oz Mexican pork chorizo
- 2 lb pork sirloin, cut into 1 inch pieces
- 1 Tbsp canola oil
- 1 medium onion, diced
- 1 Serrano pepper, minced
- 1 to 2 chipotle chiles, minced
- 1 Russet potato, peeled and sliced into bite size pieces
- 1 green plantain, sliced into bite size pieces
- 3 Roma tomatoes, diced
- 12 oz Mexican clear beer

- ⅛ cup Worcestershire sauce
- 2 tsp cumin
- ½ Tbsp oregano
- 1 tsp pepper
- Salt to taste
- 1/3 cup cilantro, chopped
- 1 cup crushed chicharrones, pork cracklins (pork rinds)

In your Discada (or extra large frying pan) cook bacon until crisp. Add the garlic and chorizo, and cook for 3 minutes. If you are using the wok shaped discada you can shift bacon and chorizo to a ring and create a well of oil to cook and fry the additional ingredients.

Turn the heat up, add the pork sirloin and cook until nicely browned and seared in most spots. If you need, add 1 Tbsp of oil.

Add the onion, Serrano, chipotle, potato, plantain and tomato, cook for 5 minutes.

Add the beer, chicken broth (as desired), and stir well to combine. When it comes to a boil, reduce heat and stir in the Worcestershire sauce, cumin, oregano, and pepper. Taste for salt before adding anymore.

Stirring now and then, cover and cook at a low simmer for 45 to 55 minutes, until the sauce reduces and becomes thick.

Add the cilantro and chicharrones to the top before serving.

Serve with warmed tortillas and salsa,

COMPETITION COOKERS AND PRO ACCESSORIES

Backyard BBQ enthusiasts can really learn a few tricks from competition cookers when it comes to hardware like top notch smokers and gadgets.

These days you'll see a lot of hard core competitive cookers using a specially made smoker called the Backwoods Competitor from a company called Backwoods Smokers. The takeaway here is you can get very consistent results with a well built air tight smoker. If you use only charcoal or cook in KCBS or Memphis in May sanctioned events or groups that only allow using wood or charcoal this model could be perfect for you. The cooking is done with efficient use of charcoal and a great chimney system.

It actually covers the meat from top to bottom. And it exits through the bottom of the chimney. So the outlet stack is actually at the bottom of the cooking chamber. And it also has a three and a half gallon water tank here for adding moisture and flavor.

These smokers feature heavy duty latches and seals and are built for competition. At 350 pounds it's ready to mount on a small trailer. With over 3000 square inches of cook space, it can accommodate most all levels of competition other than whole hogs. It retails for about 4000 dollars.

Many teams will take this type of smoker to the next level with a remote controlled blower add on. The most popular brands are the BBQ Guru and The Stoker. Kit can be purchased for around two to five hundred dollars.

Carolina Pit master's founder Jack Waiboer is a fan of the gadgets, "The BBQ Guru is really neat... you set your temperature to what your target temperature is and it gets your oven temperature up to that target and holds it there with a fan motor down on the bottom. It also has the meat probe and an alarm. When it hits your target, it will regulate temperature inside the oven to keep the meat at that temperature. If you're cooking to 195° it will hold it there when it gets there" says Waiboer.

With a charcoal fired smoker these controllers use an electric blower and remote control so they still fall within most competition guidelines.

The value in a Stoker is that you can run two or three different cookers off of your Stoker, and it has computer capabilities, so you can run your cooker off an iPhone or a laptop computer. You can control the up and down of the cooker all computerized.

When you get your system down and timing just right, it's hard to beat the solid construction of a cooker like the Backwoods Smoker and the hi-tech addition of a controller. But after spending all that money, you better win.

Chapter 3

FUEL the FLAME

" I grill therefore I am. "
– Alton Brown

Chapter 3

GAS vs CHARCOAL vs WOOD:

Some purists believe gas cooked 'QUE isn't real BBQ. I would say that's half right. I do think BBQ should have the aroma of wood smoke. Charcoal will do. But I also think adding a smoker box with some wood chips on a gas burner is almost as good and a lot less work. I was lucky enough to be raised in the suburbs of Chicago with a natural gas line fed grill in the backyard. Looking back that was really a treat. Propane tanks are cumbersome to fill, and the safety valves on the connections to the burners are often overly sensitive making for insufficient gas flow. Direct natural gas lines seem to alleviate even more hassle but are not maintenance free. I found a new respect for the complexities of natural gas burners while adjusting an indoor gas fire place. After simply adjusting the decorative ceramic logs the mantle became covered in soot. Moving the fake logs from their scientifically gas-flow designed placement caused an issue I simply couldn't imagine. The soot – from clean natural gas- was unbelievably hard to clean off the fireplace mantle and caked onto the logs. I don't want to think of it on my food. In short; don't tamper with the manufacturer's grill design. Still it's hard to beat a gas grill (propane or not) for quick cooking convenience.

CHECKING THE GAS

It's happened to a lot of cookers... so it could also happen to you! You're in the homestretch of a day of prepping for the cookout. Chicken's on... and the gas on the... grill is... slowly... dying.

Running out of propane is easy to do because it's so hard to see through metal! (Although I have seen some transparent plastic tanks recently that look great.) Most of us don't have a gas gauge either.

HERE'S ONE TIP FOR YOUR NEXT COOK OUT:

You can estimate how much gas you have left in your propane tank by heating up some water to allow you to actually feel how much propane is inside.

Make sure you have enough hot water to gently heat the SIDE of the propane tank in question. Tilting the tank on a bit of an angle, pour the hot water up and down the entire side of the tank from bottom to top. The level of liquid propane inside can be determined by feeling the new temperature of the tank with your hand. Where your hot water has

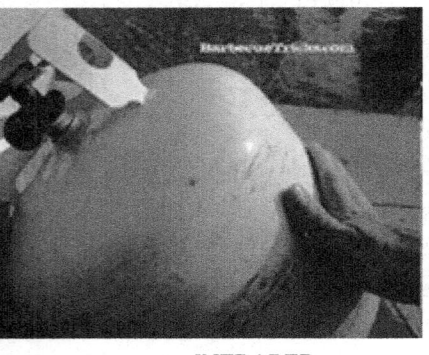

INFRARED

succeeded in heating the tank is where it's empty. Where the tank is noticeably cooler is where you have some remaining liquid propane. If there is no noticeable difference, you're probably all out.

Infrared burners can be a powerful tool in the steak lover's arsenal. These special additions to pricier gas grills use gas to heat a special ceramic plate that then emits intense searing high heat. Great for adding the heat zone that, to paraphrase Spinal Tap, "goes to eleven."

Infrared grills may be one of the newest technologies around in the age old world of BBQ, but they've been around for a few years now. TEC Grills, previously named the Thermal Engineering Corporation, claims to have started the new heating source in the early 80's.

My experience has been good with IR gas burners. It alleviates my most common headache with gas grilling which is not being able to command searing heat from weak consumer safe gas valves. They also work nicely with rotisserie models.

WE'VE GOT WOOD:

One of my earliest name changes for radio was the alias, "Bill Wood." I'm proud of my last name (Triebold), but I've been using "Bill West" so long it's easier to just stick with it.

Radio people use showbiz names for many reasons. Sometimes to throw off stalkers, but typically because a clean, simple name is easier for listeners to recall, and thus helps ratings. Once I got the morning show, I just thought it would be funny to say, "Waking up with Wood."

Interesting to me now years later, that wood is such an important ingredient in my barbecue. It's almost primal. Like a hit song, the smell of food roasting with hardwood smoke can take your mind back to special memories, moments in time and places. So below is a list of the most common barbecue and smoking woods with their most popular pairings. Feel free to adjust to infuse your favorite memory.

There are all different ways to add smoke to meat and barbecue. You don't need a true smoker with one dedicated use: smoke. I got my start smoking ribs on a regular propane gas grill. The trick is to keep the temperature low (on a gas grill this was accomplished by only having one burner lit and the meat off set on the other side of the grill and then adding your favorite wood flavor by placing wood chips, or potentially wood chunks in the mix.) Most likely you could use a smoker box – some grills are equipped with a slide-in smoker drawer/wood chip drawer these days. It is very easy to simply create a tinfoil pouch of wood chips and place the pouch directly under the grill grate on top of the burner.

Just avoid clumping all the wood chips in one place. A good trick is to spread them out or create a tube with some wood chips soaked in water for slower burning.

Smoking wood for barbecue is a must if you are cooking low and slow. The only question is "what kind of BBQ wood do you use?"
The answer is a matter of taste and what is available. In the Southeast, the mainstay is Hickory. In Texas, it's all about Mesquite. Some swear by Oak or the sweet smell of Apple wood. To make it even more complicated, others will mix a combination of woods or use aged oak whiskey barrels!

Go local? In South Carolina, our indigenous wood would be pecan. But hickory reminds me of real Carolina 'Cue as it makes me think of walking into work on Houston Northcutt Blvd and smelling the early morning hickory burning at Melvin's BBQ just down the block. Mesquite means Tex-Mex to me as I worked in my early years supplementing a shaky radio career waiting tables at The Mesa Grill in Hilton Head Island, where the real mesquite wood was an essential ingredient in the fajitas and permeated my clothes and hair (when I had hair... Hey, maybe THAT'S what happened?!) on a daily basis. Like the Kenny Chesney song "I Go Back," wood aromas and primal flavors, just like a song, can take me back to people places and fond memories. It's on a deeper level than simple nostalgia.

Thanks to the Internet everything's available. Look for the best connections on the resource page at http://barbecuetricks.com.

Acacia	Mesquite family; strong good for most meats, beef, vegetables
Alder	Delicate with a hint of sweetness; good for fish, pork, poultry, light meat game birds; great with salmon
Almond	Nutty & sweet smoke flavor, light ash; good with all meats
Apple	Slightly sweet, but dense, fruity smoke flavor; good for beef, poultry, game birds, pork and ham
Apricot	Milder flavor and sweeter than hickory; good on most meats
Ash	Fast burning, light but distinctive flavor; good with fish and red meats
Birch	Medium hard wood with a flavor like maple; good with pork and poultry
Cedar	Used for plank cooking. Typically for salmon; try shingles too
Cherry	Slightly sweet, fruity smoke flavor; good with all meats
Cottonwood	Very subtle in flavor; good on most meats
Grape Vines	Aromatic, similar to fruit woods; good with all meats
Grapefruit	Medium smoke flavor with a hint of fruitiness; excellent with beef, pork, and poultry
Hickory	Pungent, smoky, bacon-like flavor, the most common wood used; good for all smoking, especially pork and ribs – most popular grilling wood in the South
Lemon	Medium smoke flavor with a hint of fruitiness; excellent with beef, pork, and poultry
Lilac	Very light, subtle with a hint of floral; good with seafood and lamb
Maple	Mild smoky, somewhat sweet flavor; good with pork, poultry, cheese, vegetables and small game birds
Mesquite	Strong, earthy flavor, most meats, especially beef, most vegetables – most popular wood to use in Texas
Mulberry	Sweet smell and reminds one of apple; beef, poultry, game birds, pork, and ham

Wood	Description
Nectarine	The flavor is milder and sweeter than hickory; good on most meats
Oak	The second most popular wood, heavy smoke flavor, red oak is considered the best by many Pit masters; good with red meat, pork, fish and heavy game
Orange	Medium smoke flavor with a hint of fruitiness; excellent with beef, pork, and poultry
Peach	Slightly sweet, woodsy flavor; good on most meats
Pear	Slightly sweet, woodsy flavor; poultry, game birds and pork
Pecan	More like oak than hickory, but not as strong; good on most meats
Pimento	Spicy similar to mesquite, the wood of the allspice (pimento berry) which is the chosen wood for jerk chicken
Plum	Milder and sweeter than hickory; good on most meats
Walnut	Very heavy smoke flavor, usually mixed with lighter wood, like Pecan or Apple - can be bitter if used alone or not aged; good with red meats and game
Whiskey Barrel	Aged oak from Jack Daniels

PELLET POWER

One of my favorite forms of cooking with wood is by using a pellet cooker. The pellets are food grade compressed wood. The usual hardwood selections are available, and they are a great way to add some "tech" to your BBQ. Although the pellet cookers need to be plugged in (to power a blower and auger), the fuel source is still considered wood. Beware not all pellets are food grade. Some pellets are only intended for home heating units.

GETTIN' TWIGGY WITH IT

Don't limit your barbecue to just smoking with hickory and mesquite. Try experimenting with rosemary and basil twigs. If you happen to grow fresh basil during the summer months, you'll likely find that you have a dry bush of twigs as winter nears. Not good looking... but good for cooking!

Use the completely dried twigs to add flavor to your next cook out. Soak the twigs as you would any wood chips and use them to add that secret basil flavor to pork chops or a good London broil. Enjoy a cold one while your buddies argue over what wood you're using!

Similarly, Rosemary can make for a handy homegrown BBQ secret ingredient. A large rosemary bush can be trimmed to provide aromatic smoke or flavor packed kebab skewers.

Grilling fruit? Sugar cane sticks can be utilized as Kebab skewers for a subtle burst of added flavor.

PLANKS FOR NOTHING

Try your hand cooking on cedar planks right on the grill. Tip: Save a buck or ten the next time you plank grill salmon. Bypass Williams Sonoma for the pricey planks. Head to your local "Lumber Depot" and pick up a bundle of inexpensive untreated planks under or cedar shingles. The blog threemanycooks.com says their bundle for $25 bucks was enough to cook 65 Fish. Thinner than typical planks but perfect for whole sides of skin-off salmon.

JERK SECRET

Pimento wood is the smoking wood of Jerk and carribean flavors. If you can't locate pimento wood, you can substitute pimento berries. You probably have some in your cupboard already as its common name is allspice.

COAL vs. CHARCOAL vs. LUMP

Charcoal is a popular fuel source for BBQ in the form of compressed briquettes. There is a notable difference between coal and charcoal. Coal is a fossil fuel that is soft, brownish black and has been used as an energy resource. However, typical bituminous coal burns too dirty to use for food. A cleaner burning, premium type, called "Anthracite" coal is used in special ovens like Grimaldi's Pizza's coal fired pizza ovens. Grimaldi's ovens can heat up to 1,200° F and can use up to 100 lbs of coal a day. This "clean coal" is very hard and compact, produces no soot and has enough of a sheen that it is often called "black diamond." It produces no smoke when used. It is used in pizza ovens because it burns hotter than wood - Around 13,500 BTU per pound of Anthracite coal. Still, Anthracite coal is different than charcoal, and not used in at home barbecues.

BBQ Charcoal is created by carbonization of true hard wood pieces. Hardwood lump charcoal is said to burn hotter than charcoal briquettes. Unlike briquettes, lump has no fillers or binders. It's simply charred wood that creates little ash, but sometimes can. It produces snap crackles and pops. However, briquettes made from sawdust and wood chips have a more consistent and reliable burn rate. The production of briquettes was actually popularized by Henry Ford, using wood and sawdust byproducts from car manufacturing. Ford Charcoal later became the Kingsford Company.

Some Pit masters claim a fifty-fifty blend of briquettes and hardwood lump charcoal is the perfect combination of flavor, smoke, heat and consistent burn.

MEASURING BRIQUETTES

Sometimes "recipes" call for a specific volume of charcoal (like 5 quarts). One way to measure is by using a half gallon milk jug.
½ gallon (milk jug) = 2 quarts
1 quart = 16 briquettes
1 gallon = 64 briquettes
1 weber chimney = 5 quarts
1 weber chimney = 80 briquettes

Match light or fuel soaked easy lighting charcoal is convenient, but most people can taste a difference. Sometimes labeled "ready to light" the charcoal is pre-soaked with fuel and can give food a hint of a chemical taste.

I also suggest avoiding lighter fluid in starting charcoal. Instead use a simple charcoal chimney. This process is much easier than you would think and a typical chimney lights with as little as three balled up sheets of newspaper. If newspapers are "extinct" by the time you read this, I also suggest cubes of paraffin wax. Weber makes a product called lighter cubes, and they work like a charm to start a chimney of charcoal easy with zero aftertaste.

Gary House of Cooking-Outdoors.com offers up some charcoal insight earlier in chapter 2. Don't miss his take on controlling the heat for Dutch ovens.

COCONUT CHARCOAL

Feeling exotic? "Coconut shell charcoal" is a type of charcoal made out of: Coconut h made out of coconut husks, and is considered "environmentally friendly" because no trees are cut down in the manufacturing process. It is rather unusual in the states, but it has been popular for ages in Indonesia and used to fire many a saté grills in places like Thailand. If you have a small grill, coconut charcoal can be a great choice as it burns fairly hot, is quick to light, and typically comes in small pieces. Asian street vendors are the top consumers. You'll rarely spot this charcoal in brick and mortar stores in America, but it is available online. Check our resources page for best price.

LIGHTING A CHARCOAL CHIMNEY

These days everyone is focused on all natural and being green. Well, ditching the lighter fluid is a nice step towards cleaning out that fuel in your food. It's definitely safer than squirting fluid onto burning coals (you know you've seen it done). It's easy enough to tackle in four steps:

Load your charcoal chimney. Turn chimney upside down and load (the small bottom chamber) with newspaper – loosely rolled or balled. Three full sheets should suffice. Turn right side up and fill with briquettes (no need to overfill with more than you need).

Place chimney on a stable charcoal grill grate and ignite newspaper through lower holes. The charcoal should ignite slowly.

Wait as the coals fully ignite and burn off any impurities. After about 15 minutes the coals should display a fine white ash.

Use gloves (and no flip flops!) and pour the hot coals onto additional coals (As needed on the lower grill grate. The coals will burn for around an hour. Set the chimney somewhere safe (it's hot).

THE REST/FUEL

There are a few more fuel options that don't fit the above parameters. Electricity is easy to use, but I would suggest an electric smoker over a George Foreman Grill. My first smoker was a simple electric powered bullet smoker by Brinkmann that held a nice low and slow 225° temperature. The addition of wood chips and chunks made for a fantastic end product.

I have also more recently discovered the magic of pellet cookers like the Traeger line of smokers and grills. These smokers can hold a steady temperature by feeding a thermostat controlled fire pot with a stream of tiny compressed hardwood pellets. The fire is intense in a small chamber under the grill grate and indirect deflector plate. The variety of available flavored wood is also exciting. These pellet cookers have caused a bit of a stir in competitions as they usually are still judge and contest "approved" even in competitions that disallow gas and electric because ultimately these cookers heat and cook with wood. I'm a fan.

Wood Smoke "Flavors"

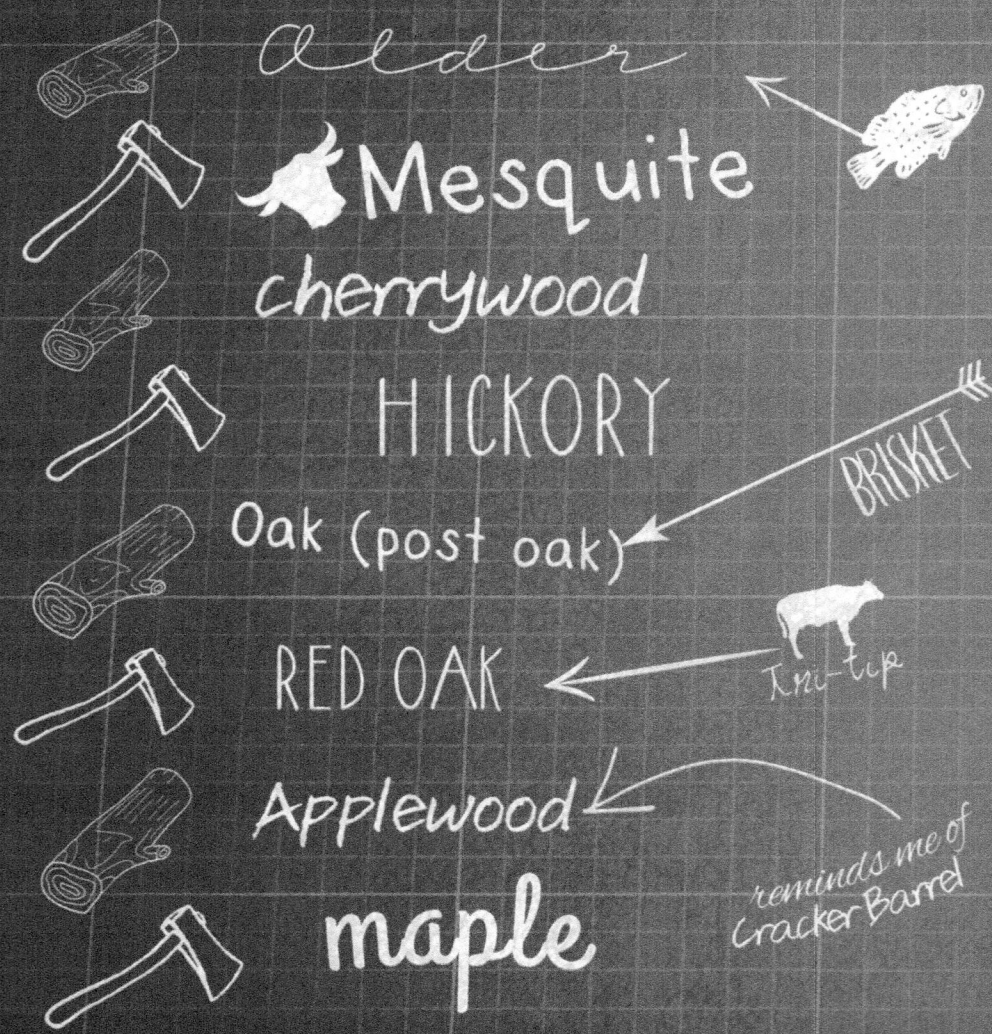

Alder ← 🐟

🐂 Mesquite

cherrywood

HICKORY ← BRISKET

Oak (post oak) ←

RED OAK ← Tri-tip

Applewood ↙

maple *reminds me of Cracker Barrel*

Chapter 4

METHODS and MEATS

" No matter how tough the meat may be, it's going to be tender if you slice it thin enough. "

– Guy Fieri

Chapter 4

The methods pit masters use on their craft often seem strange to the backyarder. Indeed there are things that a pro competition cook will do that you wouldn't care about doing at home. The meat cuts used may have been chosen based on pleasing a judge, not a "normal" person. Here are a few universal tips and tricks that can be used by us all- competition and backyarders alike.

Great BBQ requires planning and patience – start with the end in mind... have all your ingredients ready... and have your cooking process mapped out with plenty of time to allot for: slow cooking, rest time, and presentation. You want everything close at hand – your filet could be overcooked by the time you run to get the sauce from back in the kitchen, so a well executed plan will make your dinner a success.

<u>Trimming the Meat</u> - When it comes to trimming brisket, chicken, or ribs, there are different approaches when you're cooking for judges or for yourself. Sometimes competition cooks will over trim to maximize bark creation and minimize visually unpleasant bits of fat and skin. Typically most of the trimming is cosmetic. For the backyarder, fat is flavor, and you'll want to leave it on.

St Louis style Ribs are created by trimming a full slab of spare ribs to one uniform rectangular strip of bones. I love the look, but the flap of meat at the end of the ribs towards the belly that you trim off is my personal favorite morsel from the entire animal. If you do feel the need to trim it off to create a St. Louis cut, make sure you still smoke up these "rib tips" at least as a chef's snack.

THE "MONEY MUSCLE"

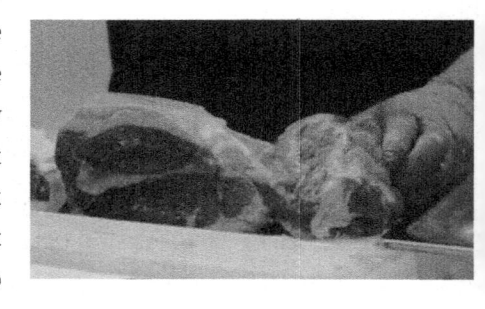

It's a Boston butt's secret weapon. If you've ever judged a BBQ contest you may be familiar with what's called "the money muscle." It is thusly named because a lot of competitive cookers think it's the best tasting part of the Boston Butt (or pork butt) and is essential on winning the top level money in high level cook-offs. In the backyard, no one really cares too much about this morsel, but it's still fun to take a closer look. How do you find the money muscle? Look at the opposite end of the butt from the bone. It is tube shaped (with striations and stripes). You can usually notice the bands of fat evenly spaced along the muscle. We're holding it in both photos here. Two whole buts are shown side by side in the second photo below.

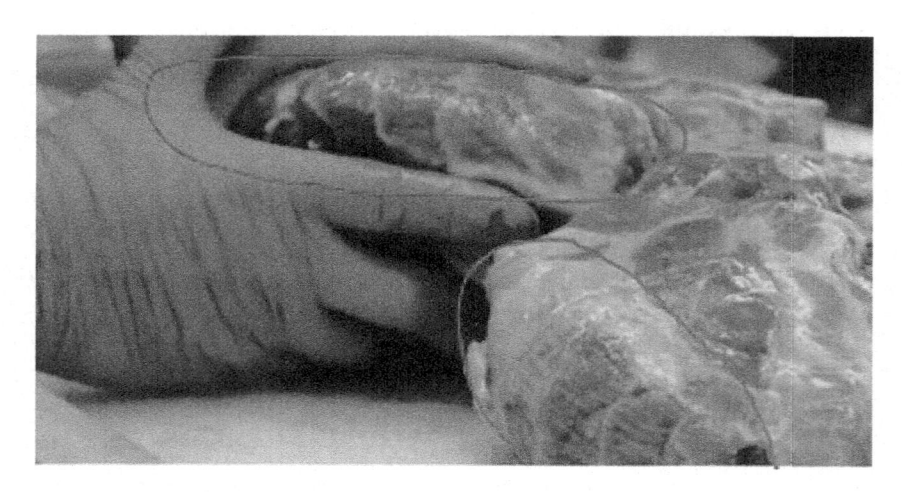

When fully cooked, that fat should easily melt away and render to provide almost a mini loin that cookers will slice and present in a blind box for competition. It's located high on the pork shoulder (read "high on the hog") and is the beginning of the loin.

That muscle just doesn't get worked much, so it's super tender.

Cookers will also promote bark creation around the money muscle by trimming around the muscle and using a good rub. Some competitions will disallow full separation from the rest of the butt while cooking, so often it is carved so as to still be connected.

"You have to trim it up so it's nice and round and it's kinda like a little loin. The great cooks use that muscle to really showcase their meat", according

to champion, Pit master Jack Waiboer.

The money muscle will cook faster than the rest of the butt (shoot for 180° for the muscle 195° for the rest of the butt). Once done, the log shaped muscle can be sliced into medallions and presented beautifully in the turn in box. The addition of a good bark on the succulent meat is a combination that wins over judges (especially in the tenderness category).

TENDERIZING

We use a few methods to tenderize tougher cuts of meat. Three of our favorites are meat mallets, marinades, and cutting against the grain.

- A meat mallet can be a fun way to pound chewy fibers into submission. Thick slabs of beef like a flavorful flank steak can take a beating and still retain a nice appearance after marinades and cooking.

- Try a marinade to soften and break down fibers with acidic ingredients as well as flavor enhancements.

- Cut against the grain of the muscle fiber. The grain is most detectable in cuts like flank, skirt, and the flat of a brisket.

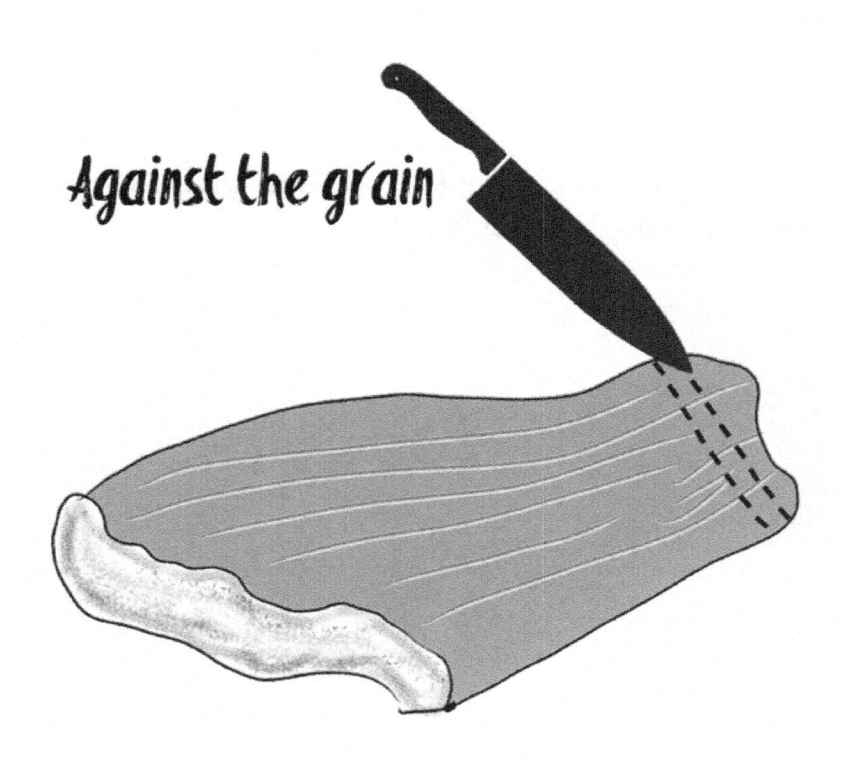

MARINADE

Marinades can pull double duty when it comes to preparing your meat. Not only will it add flavor but it also works to tenderize tougher cuts. A tenderizing marinade will need to have an acidic ingredient or natural tenderizing enzyme (like papaya or pineapple). The rest of the magic all depends on the time and the cut of meat. Steaks and larger cuts of beef can marinate for 6 to 24 hours. But fish and seafood only need 15 - 30 minutes.

Marinade Tips:

- Use your refrigerator to marinate rather than at room temperature.
- If you plan to baste with the marinade or use it in a sauce, reserve an amount prior to making contact with the meat.
- Pat dry meat after marinating to permit uniform browning and better crust.

BRINE

Salt is at the center of a brine. Different than a marinade (that tenderizes with acidic qualities and enzymes) a brine uses salt and seasonings dissolved in water to make full contact with the food surface in a uniformed concentration. In his book "Ratios" author Michael Ruhlman describes the definitive ratio or formula for a brine as 20 parts water to 1 part salt. This is a 5% salt solution. This "magic" formula has the power to soak flavor into the core fiber of the muscle. But be careful not to over brine or over salt.

Standard Brine:
20 oz Water (2 ½ cups)
1 oz Morton's kosher salt (2 Tbsp)

Quadrupled:
80 oz water (10 cups)
4 oz kosher salt (½ cup)

Keep in mind different types of salt measure differently. Morton's Kosher salt is said to have a very close volume to weight correlation. A half oz equals one Tbsp by volume. However, Diamond Kosher differs considerably.

¼ cup table salt =
¼ cup * plus 2 Tbsp * Morton's Kosher salt =
½ cup Diamond Crystal Kosher salt

Combine salt and water and heat until salt is dissolved. Remove from heat and allow to cool. Refrigerate and chill before adding meat or vegetables.

Brining Vessel Tricks:

- Use large Ziplock bags for chicken and turkey parts
- Use clean and empty cooler for the whole turkey
- Use large soup pot for whole or butterflied/spatchcocked chicken
- Use "Blue Ice" type ice packs to keep your brining solution chilled without diluting longer brines too large for the refrigerator.

POULTRY BRINE

This simple brine is perfect for a savory three or four pound chicken. It makes about a gallon of brine and also works just fine on cuts of pork.

- **10 cups apple juice**
- **6 cups water**
- **1 cup Kosher salt**
- **¼ cup brown sugar**
- **¼ cup white sugar**

Combine all of the above in a large soup pot and stir. Warm slowly, working up to medium heat until all sugar and salt fully dissolve. Let cool and chill in refrigerator. When cold, add meat and allow to soak/brine for twelve hours or more. Less for smaller cuts. Rinse before adding additional rubs or seasoning using caution not to over salt.

One additional note on everyday poultry. The birds we buy in the super marts are often already "enhanced" during packaging. Some consider this already brined as there is sodium and liquid to preserve (and add weight). The USDA requires disclosure of enhancements in the fine print. I believe this addition makes brines less effective but our acceptance of added salts over the years will make the additional level of salt still acceptable to taste. Use your own judgement.

INJECTIONS

Injections are another way to tenderize and add flavor deep into large cuts of meat. Most common in Cajun turkey and competition pork butts and even beef brisket.

Trick: inject from the inside of the cavity of the bird. Let the skin seal in the juices.

BUTT INJECTION

This simple injection is perfect for a competition pork butt or pork shoulder. It makes about 3 cups. The Tender Quick helps to enhance flavor, tenderize, and promote a pink color.

- **1 cup apple juice**
- **2 Tbsp Kosher salt**
- **½ cup water**
- **¼ cup quality Worcestershire sauce**
- **¼ cup Morton's Tender Quick**
- **½ cup brown sugar**
- **¼ cup apple cider vinegar**
- **2 Tbsp soy sauce**
- **1 tsp cayenne pepper**

Combine all of the above in a large bowl or vessel suitable for an injection needle. Stir until completely dissolved. Add ingredients as you like for deeper flavor, but beware of any spice or ingredient that will not dissolve and could clog the small hole in the injector needle.

BEEF BRISKET INJECTION

Brisket is best kept simple. However, for competitions, the pit masters pull out all the stops. The competition is all about the first bite and making it count. Use high quality beef and the additional ingredients in this injection will heighten the beefiness to another level. It makes about 3 cups. Again, Tender Quick helps to enhance flavor, tenderize, and promote a pink color.

- **1 cup beef broth**
- **1 Tbsp beef paste**
- **1 cup water**
- **2 Tbsp quality Worcestershire sauce**
- **¼ cup Morton's Tender Quick**
- **½ cup brown sugar**
- **2 cloves finely minced garlic**
- **1 onion minced**

Bill West • 75

Combine all the above in a pot and simmer briefly until all are mixed. Allow to cool and strain suitable for injection needle. Add ingredients as you like for deeper flavor but as I said above, beware of any spice or ingredient that will not dissolve and could clog the small hole in the injector needle.

CAJUN TURKEY INJECTION

Don't let the Cajun title scare you. The heat behind this tasty injection can be tempered by backing off the cayenne in the seasoning. But you shouldn't need to as it is not as potent as you might think after a long cook.

- **½ Stick of Butter (4Tbsp)**
- **1 cup unsalted chicken broth**
- **½ tsp ground white pepper**
- **Salt**
- **4 tablespoons Cajun seasoning (commercial brand)**
- **2 Tbsp white wine**

HERE'S THE RUB

Rubs are an important part of the barbecue experience. The spices in barbecue are layered on at different times of the process. After marinades (if there is a marinade or brine) you can include a rub. A rub is typically intended to be literally rubbed into the surface of the meat to penetrate deeper into the meat. Proceed with caution as all rubs are created differently with salt and spice that could be too intense if layered on too thick and then rubbed in. Some rubs should be dusted on and rubbed in sparingly; especially thinner cuts. Roasts and larger cuts are pretty forgiving.

The bark is a beautiful thing. Many people can't quite put their finger on what they love about barbecue...Upon deeper questioning it seems that what people really love is the umami flavor of charred meat (and veggies too) baked in with spices and fats to create a nice savory crust. Competition teams aim to have a little bit of bark on every piece in their turn in box for turn-in. With meat, part of the bark is the browning effect known as the "Maillard Reaction" discovered by a French doctor, Louise Camile Maillard, in 1910.

A good rub can enhance your bark, but it's worth noting that sometimes all you need is salt pepper, smoke, and time. Ask the best Texas brisket pit master. Less is more.

THE SMOKE RING

It's a pit master's point of pride -- that beautiful deep rustic red outer layer of the meat that is so tantalizing it's considered a badge of honor... the pit master's Smoke Ring. It does not mean rare or undercooked; it means roasted low and slow and smoked to perfection.

A beautiful smoke ring is actually formed through a chemical reaction. It is nitrogen and chemicals in wood smoke reacting with the surface of the meat. In all honesty, I'm not convinced the actual creation of a ring tastes any different... But it's always noticed, appreciated and just looks grea,t so Here is how to achieve it:

- First, start with lower temps: Start extra low and slow....When your meat tops 145 °, bark forms, and the chemical reaction ends so if you want a smoke ring, ramp it up slower... After that, you can throw it in the oven for all that matters.

- Second, makes sure it's wet: Keep it moist with a waterpan or baste/sop with a mop sauce for first half of cook time until about 145°.

- Third, trim: Trim fat as a smoke ring will probably not form or penetrate fat if too thick.

- Fourth, wood fire: Even more so than just smoke, actual fire really helps the chemical reaction in the smoke & meat.

- Lastly, salt: Morton's Tender Quick is a curing salt with nitrites and nitrates that you can use before cooking (Use it mixed in a rub sparingly as a little goes a long way. You could instead rub on and rinse off excess prior to cooking). It forces the chemical reaction on the surface of the meat. It's our secret ingredient for getting a smoke ring. There's also a product called Fab that is out there, or you can take a more natural route by using celery salt, celery juice, and ground celery seed in your rub and that has a good amount of naturally occurring nitrates as well.

4TH REVISION BBQ TRICK RUB

We use this rub on anything and everything but you may want to omit the cayenne for competition as the Cajun seasoning (I always sneeze when I use this) brings it's own heat too.

- **4 Tbsp paprika**
- ½ **Tbsp chili powder**
- ½ **Tbsp cayenne pepper (optional for heat)**
- **3 Tbsp Tony Cachere's Cajun Seasoning**
- **1 Tbsp brown sugar**
- **4 Tbsp Sugar In The Raw**
- ½ **Tbsp ground cumin**

Combine all the above in an airtight container and store in a cool dark place. Or prepare right before using. Rub on meat approximately one hour before cooking, when possible.

3rd BASE BIRD RUB

One trick for taste bud poppin' chicken is to get the seasoning and spices into the meat. The skin can act as a wet suit so use your fingers to rub this mixture under the skin into the thicker muscles of the bird. Other techniques are to "dry brine" the skin to get it crispy, removing and scraping the skin to achieve bite-through goodness, or using a wet brine.

- **3 tsp Greek seasoning (Cavender's)**
- **2 tsp Hungarian paprika**
- **1 tsp black pepper**
- **1 tsp thyme**
- **1 tsp salt (depending on Greek seasoning)**

Set your cooker for indirect heat or smoke, and a drip pan is suggested. Cook for approximately one hour at 275° - 300°, or until the internal temperature of the thickest part of the meat reaches 165°. When cut or pierced, juices should run clear. Allow for a ten minute rest.

CHILI POWDER

Arbol Chiles

One secret to livening up any recipe that calls for chili powder is to make your own. It's a trick that takes an everyday pot of chili to an award winning level — I know first hand! It's fun and easy to make. Use those dried whole chilies you see at the store (you may want to mix and match if you can't find Guajillo, Arbol or Ancho) and toast /roast them briefly in a cast iron pan. Be careful not to burn them; they go from tan to burned in moments and don't choke on the potentially potent fumes. Pull the stems and grind with cumin seeds in a blender, coffee grinder, or spice grinder. Simple and adds unbelievable flavor.

- **2 oz Ancho Chiles – dried and roasted**
- **2 oz Guajillo Chiles – dried and roasted**
- **1 oz Chile de Arbol – dried and roasted**
- **5 Tbsp Cumin seeds – toasted and ground**
- **2 Tbsp granulated garlic**
- **4 Tbsp oregano**
- **4 Tbsp smoked paprika**

Toast whole dried peppers and cumin seeds in a skillet until they start to brown slightly. Let cool, and grind to a powder.

SPICE TIPS

How do you store your spices? With a little care, you can make your spices pop just a bit more according to Cheyenne Ledyard from Etsy's, The BBQ Pantry. The tips and tricks – paraphrased below (see them all on my YouTube Channel) are worth noting:

1. Get Toasty. Toast Your Spices and maximize the potency. This releases oils and flavor.
2. Stay cool. Never store the spices above a stove. Heat degrades flavor.
3. Don't store spices too long. Keep it fresh.
4. Use your freezer. Dark and sealed dry. Keep them in the dark. Sunlight degrades flavor too. See tip 2.
5. Toast It. A quick heating in a non stick pan can release and brighten the oils in your favorite spices.

SPICE TRAVEL

Recently my family traveled to Florida and stayed in a condo with a full kitchen but, of course, there were no pantry items available for a rental. Have you ever had to buy twenty dollars worth of salt, pepper, and other spices you probably already have at home?

Here's a simple solution... If you do a lot of traveling, you'll save some money by having a portable handy spice rack ready to go. This trick comes compliments of Chef/Owner, Paul Stewart of Palmetto Bay Sunrise Cafe on Hilton Head Island, SC, and it's a keeper. He says to use one of those inexpensive "day of the week" pill dispensers to act as your seven spice rack. It may not hold enough rub for a BBQ competition, but it can probably store enough for a weekend at the beach. Our suggestion: keep it in a zip-lock bag in the suitcase to keep your underwear from smelling like garlic... unless of course, you're into that sort of thing.

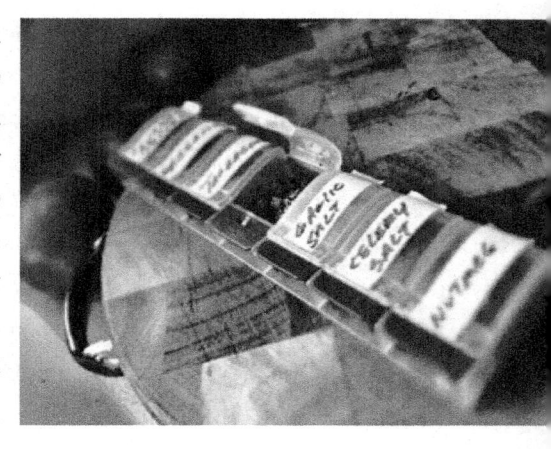

REVERSE SEAR

There are hundreds of ways to cook a steak. Most BBQ aficionados and backyarders keep it simple. Fire up high heat and sear the rib-eye and hope the middle is still good. The traditional thought is that the initial sear "Locks in juices." The reality is the sear will not lock in anything... it's kind of BS... in fact, we've all seen a seared steak still pool with juices.

But the fast sear is fine for most - honestly, I could eat a steak no matter if you cooked it in a crock pot... even when it's bad - it's still pretty good....but lately there has been talk of a reverse sear method. Here's the deal:

It's basically the opposite of that fast sear and bake. In this case, you START the steak off low and slow - between 250° and 300° on indirect heat. You grill until the internal temperature reaches a temperature that is about ten degrees BELOW your final desired internal temp.

If you want it around 150° Medium - (USDA may differ) target 140° with a quick read thermometer. Then pull it off the heat for a few minutes until it just starts to drop below 140°. That's your cue to fire up the high heat or searing burner and blast it on both sides to achieve the charred caramelization and crust. Pull and enjoy.

Some experts say the low and slow reverse sear method gives you a more tender steak allowing natural enzymes some additional time to do some magic. Most say it wont affect flavor all that much - but I believe you do end up with a better char and crust.

TAKE A REST

After you've been slaving all day over the hot coals grilling, you need a rest, and the meat does too. One of the hardest things for me to do is to enforce a ten minute rest on the meat. Pulling the meat off the grate and stopping the heat, tenting with foil, and allowing for just a 10-15 minute rest will stop the cooking process gently, so that when you make the first cut, all those valuable and flavorful juices won't be wasted on your cutting board.

ZONED OUT

Whether you are cooking on gas, charcoal or even a stick burner you will want to maintain different "zones" to control your cook. On gas grills separate knobs may handle the job with different burners being utilized. On charcoal grills you can create differing heat levels by layering charcoal in three different depths across the grill grate. I also recommend a drip pan under the cool level to avoid any surprise flare ups. A disposable pie pan or larger banquet pans work great.

If you don't have an accurate thermometer on each zone on the grill, you can make a good estimate by using the hand test. Simply try to hold your palm five or six inches above the coals.

- High Heat – You can bear to hold your hand in place for one or two seconds.

- Medium Heat – You can bear to hold your hand in place for three to four seconds. Approximately 375°.

- Low or Smoking Heat – You should be able to hold your hand in place for about six seconds. Smoking temp is 225° - 250°.

HOLD ON TO YOUR LID

If you're trying to decide between lid up or lid down, use this guide: If the food is thicker than your palm, close the lid. You want bigger pieces to be surrounded by the heat so that the meat cooks quicker and more evenly. The larger it is, the less you want it just blasted up on one side from below. But if the food is thinner than your fingers or middle of your hand, leave the lid up. You can keep a better eye on the grill and vegetables will stay crisp without steaming and getting soggy if you leave the lid up.

BBQ BLUEPRINT
cheat sheet

MEAT	Smoking Temp.	Internal Target	USDA Recommen[ded]
 Beef	225-275F	195-205F	145F
 Pork	225-275F	195-205F	145F
 Chicken	250-300F	165F	165F
 Turkey	250-300F	165F	165F
 Fish	225-250F	145F	145F

TEMPERATURE CHECK

There are a lot of ways to check the doneness temperature of your barbecue. Thermo pen instant read thermometers get high marks when tested for reliability for meat thermometers. However, they cost over 80 bucks, and there will still be many times you won't have any sort of meat thermometer handy. That's OK. We've discovered what we call our "OK HANDY" method of checking for meat doneness. It's especially handy for steaks and thicker cuts of beef.

First off here are some temperature guidelines:

- Rare steak 125° to 130°F
- Medium Rare 130° to 135°F
- Medium 135° to 145°F
- Medium Well 145° to 150°F
- Well done 150° to 155°F or higher

Here's how to know when to pull it off the grill with the tools you always have with you…your hands!

First off loosen up your hand. Massage, stretch and shake one hand loose so that your thumb and it's muscles are fully relaxed.

- Touch the round base of your thumb on the relaxed hand. This soft resistance and feel is similar to the texture of a very medium rare steak.
- Now – make the "OK" sign (don't pinch… just close your thumb and forefinger together) and now touch and feel the firmness at the base of your thumb. This texture is more similar to a medium-rare steak.
- Next, touch your thumb to your middle finger. This firmer resistance is similar to the texture of a medium steak.

- Finally, touch your thumb to your pinky. The very firm (some would say tough, and my wife would translate, ruined) texture at the base of your thumb is closest to a well-done steak.

Of course you will run into problems with this OK Handy method on pork ribs so instead, reach for a simple toothpick. First, the bones start to stick out when things are just about done. Then a toothpick when poked into the flesh of the ribs will push in and pull out very easily when fully cooked to Pit master's standards. Again, the best way to know is to use an instant read meat thermometer… but now you will always have a few methods handy.

five major BBQ groups

brisket

chicken

ribs

butt = shoulder

whole hog

Chapter 5

FIVE
MAJOR BBQ
Food Groups

> "Part of the secret of a success in life
> is to eat what you like
> and let the food fight it out inside."
> **— Mark Twain**

Chapter 5

The methods pit masters use on their craft often seem strange to the Backyarder. Indeed there are things that a pro competition cooks need to worry about that the backyard either doesn't want to or shouldn't need to even consider. Does the smoke ring make a difference in flavor? Probably not. Do you have to make it pop in flavor with one, and only one, bite? Not at home. Plus at home, there are no rules, and you don't have to frame it in a Styrofoam to-go box. Nonetheless, there are still five major meat groups that are the most popular, not only in competition cooking but also simply in world barbecue and in the backyard.
They are:

- Ribs - usually spare ribs, and almost always pork
- Beef brisket (burnt ends too)
- Chicken
- Pork Butt or Shoulder
- Whole Hog

COMPETITION VS BACKYARD

So we already know that the burger and hotdogs are one of the most popular dishes to cook on the grill, but pit masters and backyarders all enjoy cooking big. The backyarder as well as the competition pit master works on the five biggies mentioned above to really display their prowess on the grill or smoker. The thing is, the backyarder is only judged by flavor and by friends. In the backyard, there is no turn-in time or judges. No rules. So this is where a real cook with creativity can shine.

In the competition world, the judges are trained to discriminate different categories of profiles in each of the big meats. Ratings of the four meats, or five if you do a whole hog, are on a scale of 1 to 9 and usually are subjected to 3 categories, for instance: "Appearance" which is simply how good does it look in the box? There are rules against pooling sauce or marking any meat in the box, to keep cheating non-existent. Some competitions include garnishes which can be a distraction all in itself. Parsley or lettuce pinwheels or lettuce bedding? The biggest part of appearance is the overall sheen of the meat. Is the surface perfectly lacquered? Is each rib bone uniform in size and shape? Do you have a perfect bite for all six judges?

Then there's even a smell. Many times the box will literally be passed around the table for a quick sniff - sounds kind of gross, right? But ultimately it is the taste category that moves the needle and is often times weighted as a higher point structure. It needs to pop. And it needs to pop in one bite - the first bite - for jaded judges. You'll want to showcase a bit of bark in each bite as well. You should know there is a belief, popularized by super pit master and champion, Myron Mixon, that judges like it sweet.

Finally, tenderness is a category of judging that is the trickiest to pin down. Different meats have different points where they get tender and pull apart, and sometimes pull-apart is too tender, especially in the case of fall-of-the-bone ribs. You want the meat to yield to a perfect bite, but not turn to mush. To complicate matters, you can do a lot of trickery with a tight bark on the outside of very tender meat. Judges may pull the thin slice of brisket between their fingers and look closely at how the fibers break apart. Same with pulled pork strands. If the fiber of the meat tugs all apart gently and softly with a soft edge, it is deemed tender, but if the brisket springs back like a rubber band or the pork is stringy (or heaven for bid, it's dry!) or if there is a piece of gristle in the box that they happen to grab, it is deemed tough or worse. You got one bite to make an impression. Plus you are in a lineup of six competing samples on a placemat with a numbered grid.

IS THIS CHEATING?

The sanctioned BBQ world is serious business. Maybe too serious if you've ever seen BBQ Pit Masters on TV. There are pages of detailed rules that are never really reviewed prior to competitions by judges or by cookers. Some rules are regional by nature. Like, meat categories (whole hog contests are hard to find outside the South). Others – like the rule for only using wood or charcoal as a heat source – is somewhat common. I've even seen rules against team members drinking to excess.

If you are looking to get the upper hand and bend the rules a bit, here are a few ways that competition cooks quietly get an edge. I can not condone or encourage, but do find it interesting.

1. First, start with better meat. You could use meat that the tournament provides or bring in your own grain fed premium grade organic – more tasty – better meat. There may or may not be fine print on "only using what the sponsor provides" but the rule is rarely enforced or even checked. It's more likely your meat cooler will only be checked for food safety reasons (like maintaining a cold enough temperature). I've seen teams bring in top of the line Wagyu beef brisket. It's pricey. But if it indeed tastes better, it's a real edge. A great source for highest quality brisket is on the resources page. Some winning cookers have been known to bring in secret recipe pre-brined chicken, but you can't do this if everything has to be prepped onsite.

2. Next, use electricity to help your cooking efficiency and consistency. Many big organizations (like KCBS and MIM) forbid heat sources other than wood or charcoal. Still it's within guidelines to get a little electric help. So gadgets have been designed to make charcoal (use hardwood lump for best flavor) more reliable and consistent in temperature. Look into retrofitting your smoker with an electric blower with a thermostat to stoke your fire up or down to the ideal

temperature while you play Angry Birds in the RV. Most common are the BBQ Guru and the Stoker.

3. Get the most bark for your buck. Judges like bark; that savory sweet charred crust found on great BBQ meats. Trim your pork so you have the most and best tasting bark represented. The "money muscle" is a tucked away tube of succulence on the Boston Butt that many cooks are trying to really take advantage of for it's tender texture and flavor. It's almost entirely surrounded by other parts of the butt, so if you want to combine the great meat of the money muscle and the magic of great tasting bark, you'll have to trim out the money muscle before cooking. In some competitions, it's against the rules to cook large meats in parts, so you may want to simply keep a small portion still attached to the "mother ship."

4. Cheat the smoke ring. It is absolutely expected for brisket and pork to have a nice smoke ring when turned in to judges. This is formed by a chemical reaction to the smoke over low temp and given time. Some say if you put COLD meat on the smoker from the start it will enhance the ring. We say, don't leave it to chance. Cheat the ring by adding some curing salt to your rub like Morton's Tender Quick. It's strong stuff so some cookers will coat the meat for a few hours and rinse it off before adding the tasty – bark creating rub.

5. Microwave friendly. As stated above... cooking with fuel other than wood or coal could be against the rules so why would you need a microwave? Well, judges like to bite into a warm piece of meat. They also judge on smell and warm meat will always be more fragrant than cold meat. I've personally never done this, but a fifteen second zap in the box is sometimes the perfect bump to setting your entry apart. Against the rules? Is fifteen seconds really cooking? You decide. Just silence the "beeping" and don't let Bubba's team see you doing it.

These rarely policed barbecue tricks may or may not be truly cheating the BBQ Rules. Read the fine print of your rules and let your conscience be your guide. The one rule you can not and should not bend is "marking" a box. This is where a team has a mole in the judging tent clued in on a special trait or "mark" on a turn in box. Don't try. It won't work due to rotating judges and will probably get you disqualified or marked down in appearance points. Instead, use care to really "present" your meat in the box. Follow the guidance in the rules on garnish and ask around about traditional layout. Appearance is almost always a big part of your score, and it's surprising how many cooks just plop it in the box. Pull pork (never chop) and lay out pieces in an orderly presentation. It's more important than you think.

COMPETITION FORMS

One solid way to improve the quality of your BBQ is to track your success and failures.

Most great (and winning) Pit Masters usually have a crusty and sauce stained binder filled with cook logs of previous runs. We'll provide downloadable and editable copies of these on the recourses page of BarbecueTricks.com but feel free to create your own version of this example:

BBQ Cook Log Page (example at end of chapter)
http://barbecuetricks.com/book-resources

It is also smart to head to the competition site prepared with everything you will need. There's a lot. Here's a copy of the checklist I put together to stay on track. Your needs may differ, but it's a smart reminder of the little things. Fire extinguisher included.

Competition Checklist example 1-4
http://barbecuetricks.com/book-resources

Competition Checklist

Have	Need	Cooking Supplies	Note
		Aprons	
		Ash Bucket	
		Cast Iron Skillet	
		Charcoal (Wood Lump)	
		Chimney Fire Starter	
		Cooker(s)	
		Cutting Board(s)	
		Foil Pans (Small & Large)	
		Injectors/Brine Pump	
		Insulated Bag	
		Knives	
		Lighter/Matches	
		Paper Bags	
		Pot Holders/Handle Cover	
		Propane	
		Sharpener(s)	
		Smoke Wood	
		Spatulas/Wooden Spoons	
		Spray Bottles	
		Thermometers	
		Tongs, Can Opener, etc.	
		Turkey Fryer	

Have	Need	Storage & Cleaning	Note
		Aluminum Foil	
		Aluminum Pans	
		Bleach	
		Broom	
		Coleman Sink	
		Coolers	
		Dish Rags/Scrubbers	
		Dish Soap	
		Dish Tubs	
		Gloves (Grill & Latex)	
		Grate Cleaner/Scrubbers	
		Hand Sanitizer	
		Hand Soap	
		Paper Towels	
		Plastic Wrap	
		SOS Pads/Sponges	
		Toilet Paper	
		Trash Bags	
		Water Container(s)	
		Wet Wipes	
		Ziploc Bags (1 Gal & 2 Gal)	
		10'x10' EZ Up Tent	

Have	Need	Food/Drinks/Etc.	Note
		Anything Butt Ingredients	
		Apple Cider Vinegar	
		Apple Juice	
		Beer/Adult Beverages	
		Coffee	
		Ice	
		Lettuce/Parsley	
		Marinade	
		Orange Juice	
		Rub/Slather	
		Sauce	
		Snacks	
		Sodas	
		Water	

Have	Need	Meat	Note
		Brisket (1)	
		Butts/Shoulders (2)	
		Chicken Thighs/Wings (20)	
		Ribs (3-4)	
		Whole Hog	

Have	Need	Miscellaneous	Note
		Banner	
		Batteries	
		Bucket	
		Bug Spray/Candles	
		Camera	
		Camping Coffee Pot/Cups	
		Chairs	
		Clean Cloths	
		Dry Erase Markers/Chalk	
		Dry Erase/Chalk Board	
		Duct Tape	
		Extension Cords	
		Fan	
		Fire Extinguisher (10 lb)	
		First Aid Kit	
		Flashlights/Lanterns	
		Garden Hose	
		Generator/Gasoline	
		Paper Plates/Napkins	
		Pillows/Bedding	
		Plastic Cups/Koozies	
		Plastic Silverware	
		Propane	
		Rain Gear	
		Sleeping Bags/Tent	
		Spare Cooker Parts	
		Sunblock	
		Tables & Table Covers	
		Tools/Screw Drivers/Hammer/Scissors	
		Toothbrushes/Etc.	

RIBS

We're talkin' pork for competition ribs. Primarily pork spare ribs are used, and they are trimmed to achieve a St. Louis style cut. That is with the thinner and tapered flap trimmed off to create uniformity in shape - a long rectangular slab. Next use care to peel the membrane off the inside of the rib cage so your spice rub will penetrate. Although it's optional to remove in restaurants and at home, it's a must if you are pleasing a judge (they simply see it as a negative). Proper trimming allows for each bone to be the same shape and close in size to the others.

A rib is one of the meats that is treated carefully for competition turn-in to achieve what judges consider a perfectly cut bone, which is meaty on both sides and cooked to achieve a perfect bite that can be characterized NOT as "fall off the bone" but as a bite that comes loose with a gentle tug leaving behind a bare (almost white) bone peeking thru a perfect half moon shaped bite. But really the typical backyarder likes a fall off the bone rib when it's smoked to succulence. The method to achieve succulence with smoke is as easy as 1-2-3... Or really 3-2-1.

THREE – TWO – ONE METHOD

The trick is to break down the low and slow, spare rib cooking process into three easy to remember segments of time and add in some time spent wrapped in foil. This "Three – Two – One" trick works for gas grills. Works for charcoal. Even works in an electric smoker or – gasp – the oven.

- You start with a stable low temperature on your grill while you prep the ribs – and again we're talking pork ribs here – with the rub of your choice. We like pulling the membrane off the back with a paper towel for good grip, and trimming them up "square or St Louis style."

- With the grill temp set at 225° F for the long cook, you start with 3 hours of indirect heat on the grill. This is when you are going to get all the smoke flavor, so use wood smoke via chips or chunks of wood (we like hickory or pecan) during this time.

- After this step, you then use what they call the "Texas Crutch." It has nothing to do with Texas BBQ really. Simply put, you wrap and seal the ribs in heavy duty aluminum foil. The smoke should have done most of the "flavoring" that it can in the first few hours and won't penetrate much more at this temperature. So, no more wood chips are needed. Also before wrapping, most pit masters usually add a cup of a sweet or even savory liquid to the meat. Apple juice is popular. Some spritz it out of a spray bottle; others just pour some in the foil packet. If you like sweet, it's a good time to add that layer of flavor with a sweet sauce, brown sugar or maple syrup maybe. Now you will be basically braising the ribs, and it will result in that fall off the bone experience. Try not to go too long (or too hot) in this stage- about 2 hours - or you can give the ribs a texture that becomes too mushy. In the backyard (with the exception of competition judges) most of your guests will appreciate and rave about that fall off the bone Q.

- Finally, unwrap the ribs and cook on indirect heat for 1 more hour adding layers of sauce as you allow the more dry heat to tighten up the surface of the ribs and create a firm bite. Shellac, glaze, or char for your desired finish. The more sugar in the sauce the faster it will burn, so be careful with that. By adding a nice bark, you can avoid having the meat actually fall from the bone enroute to the plate.

It's a fool proof trick for barbecue ribs that your guests will rave about. The Three - Two - One Method is a simple barbecue trick that works, and it's even easier to remember.

THE MOTHER CHURCH OF DRY RIBS

Memphis Tennessee is the home of the blues, Beale Street, Graceland, Sun Studios and of course great barbecue. Down one aromatic alleyway, it's where you can find what some meat heads say are the world's best bones: Legendary Memphis dry-rub ribs.

Dry, yet savory. Still juicy - with seasonings on top and a tangy pool of sweet vinegar sauce below. Find the dark back alley just down from the elegant Peabody Hotel and you'll discover the world-famous Rendezvous. The mother church of dry-rub Memphis style ribs.

Set with a dark back brick entrance with a black awning and neon behind a brick store in tough downtown Memphis, it's certainly not highfalutin' but you can definitely smell the charcoal wood fired smoke as you enter the dark entrance down to the famous basement. Get ready. It's not unusual to find people taking cell phone photos of their food and getting messy. Rib selfies.

Inside you can see bow-tied waiters with white shirts - the same waiters that have likely worked the room for decades -some over 40 years. The walls sport memorabilia about visits from presidents and performers alike, ranging from George Bush to Elvis

Charlie Vergos (pronounced Vargus) opened this place in 1948, and many of the traditions in the restaurant and even some of the menu items still remain in place today. The house appetizer is still a common sausage and cheese platter. And the centerpiece of the joint is the open kitchen where the slabs (note: membrane still intact) still roast in the same charcoal chute adapted ovens.

The Vergos barbecue trick is roasting the slabs one to two feet directly over high heat above hardwood charcoal... For about an hour or 30 minutes per side...then mopped with a light vinegar sauce and coated with a dusting of spices. It's called rendezvous seasoning rather than rub because it's sprinkled on and not rubbed in.

The seasoning is paprika based but also features whole celery seed, yellow mustard seeds, allspice and coriander too - get the detailed recipe at BarbecueTricks.com by searching "rendezvous."

The now coveted dry spices were influenced by Greek roots which made its way to the ribs that are still fire roasted beneath the now legendary charcoal chute.

And they go through a ton of ribs - One of the benefits of going to the restaurant in person is being able to see the magic happen in the hustle and bustle of the smoky open kitchen. Ribs are tossed on bone side down to protect the meat. The typical order comes with brown sugar and bacon baked beans and mustard-tinged coleslaw. Served on paper plates with a white cloth napkin.

The large order of ribs is about nineteen bucks and worth every penny. If you can't make it to Memphis, you can still get a taste of Rendezvous via their lucrative website at hogsfly.com where they ship ribs across the country overnight via Memphis neighbor FedEx. Yes, we have shipped them more than once!

The restaurant is closed on Sunday, so be careful how you plan your weekend.

Insider's tip: If you can plan ahead with a group, call and ask about their skillet of shrimp.

Also known as dry-rib rub this coriander and Greek influenced rub is fantastic on everything from ribs to popcorn. The real trick here is to cook the ribs hot and fast over hardwood charcoal (Royal Oak brand) and the seasoning is not rubbed in but adheres thanks to a flavorful splash of a light vinegar sauce. They also make the bold decision to leave the membrane on the back of the bones at the Memphis institution. Although the exact recipe varies from the original, here are the basics:

- **4 Tbsp American paprika**
- **4 Tbsp powdered garlic**
- **2 Tbsp mild chili powder**
- **1 Tbsp fresh ground black pepper**
- **2 tsp whole yellow mustard seed**
- **1 tsp crushed celery seed**

RENDEZVOUS RUB

- ½ Tbsp whole celery seed
- ½ Tbsp whole allspice seeds
- 1 dash ground allspice
- ½ Tbsp whole coriander seed
- ½ tsp ground coriander

For best results bloom whole seeds if available in pan over stove and grind whole seeds into a coarse rub. You may wish to crush the whole seeds in a mortar and pestle before blending. Store in an airtight container for up to a month.

DRY RIB MOP

Use this as a simple basting sauce to adhere the famous dry rub or other spices. A final splash and sprinkle (dusted evenly from above) make for an explosive dry bite.

- **2 cups pickle juice**
- **1 Tbsp sweet paprika**
- **2 Tbsp Rendezvous Rib Rub**
- **1 Tbsp red pepper flakes (optional)**

PULLED PORK

First, understand that a Pork Butt is actually the top part of the pork shoulder with shank end (the picnic shoulder) separated. Whole shoulders are sometimes used in competition but are harder to find in typical grocery stores. So the butt is really the shoulder, and the rear end is famously known as the ham.

You can use the ham for pulled pork. Some pit master's will combine ham with butts. Larry Sconyers of Sconyers Barbecue in Augusta, Georgia, is popular for exclusively using whole hams. For backyard cooking an uncured (sometimes called green) ham would be difficult to find outside a true butcher shop.

The shoulder of the pig is loaded with fatty deposits and collagen heavy muscle fibers. That's why unlike other meats, it is never prepared rare. Once you roast slowly to reach an internal temperature of 185° to over 195° to achieve pull-apart succulence, some butts are more stubborn than others and can "stall" in mid cook holding a plateau for a surprisingly long time. This is when the Pit master needs to show some restraint in lifting the lid. Opening (and cooling) the cook chamber can unintentionally add ten minutes (per "peek") to the final cook time. For most meats you want your cooker to maintain a steady 225°.

Here is where BBQ magic happens. Conventional wisdom tells us we cook meat until it is "done" (usually to USDA recommended internal temperatures). However in THIS definition of barbecue (the low and slow mind set), we need more beer. In order to achieve that pull apart texture from which "pulled pork" gets its name, you need to continue to nurse the internal temperature of the center of the pork to around 205° Fahrenheit.

THE STALL
On the way to your target temperature different cuts from different animals have been known to cook at different rates. Pit masters have told me tales of stubborn roasts that for no particular reason took hours longer than

similar cooking on the same grill grate. Some of this mystery is a part of "the stall." There is a period of time where the internal temperature of the meat will continue to rise at a predictable pace and then plateau for a bit before proceeding to doneness. The simple advice is to be patient and try not to make matters worse by opening your cooker/cooking vessel more than necessary (thus cooling the grill and exacerbating the problem as mentioned above). Be patient.

Pork butts typically take approximately one and a half hours per pound to cook. You'll need eight to twelve hours. When "done at 205" you should start to notice a tell tale "jiggle" and softer texture. The blade bone should also slide right out by hand.

Add any sugary sauces and sprays to create your best bark at the end of the process (or add after pulling).

If you have time before serving, the meat can be held for hours in a homemade "Cambro" in the form of an empty plastic cooler. Wrap the meat in foil or plastic wrap and then clean beach towels for added insulation.

BEEF BRISKET (BURNT ENDS)

The basics of beef brisket are remarkably simple if you want it to be. Salt and coarse pepper and quality meat. Pit master Christopher Hill of Melvin's Barbecue in Mt. Pleasant, South Carolina has spent a lot of time perfecting the brisket process on their cookers, and he says, "You just need simple ingredients and a great product, the beef. You need a smoker with good wood, and you need time." Melvin's uses high quality grass fed hormone free beef. Quality meat is also a trend that has made its way to the competition circuit. These days it's common for the serious competition teams to choose Top of the line premium Wagu cuts from specialty providers like Snake River (check our resource page for a few preferred providers). The higher the quality (yes, more expensive) the better the final flavor. With beef, fat equals flavor, so starting with the best from places like Snake River Farms you'll be starting at the front of the pack.

The Point and The Flat -
The brisket is a massive chuck of meat from the chest area of the cow. The whole brisket consists of a large thick and flat slab of muscle fibers that run the length of the slab as well as an attached cap of fattier meat on one end of the slab called the "point" or "deckle." Although you can find the flat sold separately in smaller portions in supermarkets; pit masters usually use the full brisket. In restaurants like Melvin's, guests in the know can request "point, fatty, or moist" or "flat, lean." For competition, the flat will be carved up, against the grain, in uniform pencil thin slices (each sauced individually for sheen as well as for the judges perfect bite). The point will also be used in competition but usually reserved for the super succulent

burnt ends. Cubes of caramelized beef and buttery, fatty, barky goodness. My spell check doesn't like the word "bark-y" but let me just tell you bark is beautiful.

Here are the simple steps:

1. Trim off hardened fat thicker than a half of an inch thick.
2. Slather the meat with an inexpensive yellow mustard to act as an adherent.
3. Coat the entire surface of the meat with a 50/50 blend of coarse kosher salt and medium coarse black pepper. It's a lot of salt and pepper but a roast this size uses it nicely.
4. Smoke at 225° indirectly using post oak (if keeping traditional) until the internal temperature reaches approximately 165°. This is usually four or five hours. Keep the cooker shut.
5. Wrap with butcher paper tightly to seal in juices and continue to cook up another 35° to an internal temperature of around 205° Fahrenheit. Then it's usually another four - five hours at cooker temperature of 225°, but smoke is no longer a factor.
6. Allow for meat to rest off heat fifteen minutes before slicing. Separate point and reserve for burnt ends if desired. Slice the flat against the grain.

BURNT ENDS

The point end of the brisket can also be served sliced. It is a twisted group of meat fibers so the grain of the meat is not as easy to follow. Often it is chunked or cubed and prepared as burnt ends. Burnt ends are said to have originated in a Kansas City restaurant as diners there started to demand the previously disregarded morsels as a sought after delicacy.

The true punch of these burnt ends will come from the beef, bark, and fat ratio you achieved with the full brisket you smoked and the spices used to create the bark. Cubed portions of the point will work best for burnt ends thanks to the high fat. Burnt ends can be prepared as savory or sweet. The recipe below is a nice blend of both.

Mix all the ingredients excluding the beef in a bowl. Spread the meat cubes evenly across a baking sheet and paint the surfaces of the meat cubes on all sides. Cook over indirect heat to render any additional fat and caramalize the sugars in the sauce. Reapply additional coatings to taste.

- 2 cups cubed smoked beef brisket (preferably point/deckle with bark on one surface)
- 1 cup Apple cider vinegar
- 2 Tbsp brown sugar
- 1 Tbsp sweet paprika
- 1 Tbsp rub
- 2 Tbsp quality Worcestershire sauce

CHICKEN

Chicken Thighs are the go to meat for competition, and it's a good thing because it is a lot easier on the wallet than other meats. Pit masters use thighs because it is far more resistant to drying out than any other part of the bird. The trick to chicken is to get the skin to cooperate with the judges' first bite (without sliding off). In competition, you'll want to cook a lot of thighs to get the perfect six or eight as needed for the judges.

Here is the secret to getting bite-through chicken skin every time.

1. According to Seth Watari of CarolinaPit masters.com cooking school, you first separate the skin of the thighs (off the meat) and chill them. Cold chicken skin is a lot easier to work with and to trim.

2. Trim the fat off the inside of the cold skin using a very sharp knife and the touch of a plastic surgeon. Some pit masters will scrape while others prefer cutting and trimming off the layer of fat.

3. Brine the chicken thighs for less than an hour. Do not brine the skin.

4. Season the uncovered thigh with a chicken rub and neatly re-apply the skin.

5. Smoke the thighs on indirect heat approximately 250° until the internal temperature of the chicken reads 165° Fahrenheit (74° Celsius) on an instant read meat thermometer.

6. Sauce, glaze, finish as a final step briefly over direct heat.

Chicken breasts are less forgiving than the dark meat of the thigh, so they are less popular on the barbecue circuit but more popular in many homes. Just remember that the white meat of the breast is a bit more resistant to rubs and marinades so you can give it more time to absorb the flavors.

How do you know it's done? The best way to determine done-ness in poultry is to use an electric instant read thermometer (check the resources page for the latest model). The Thermapen/Thermoworks instant read has historically been a very dependable favorite. Insert the thermometer probe into the thickest part of the thigh being sure to avoid touching bone. I'll usually use a second reference point in the center of a meaty breast as well. USDA and Pit masters agree on an internal temperature target of 165° F. Any juices at this point should run clear.

CRISPY SKIN (WITHOUT FRYING)

If you are looking to achieve a crispy chicken skin without frying the secret is in planning ahead.

You can first "dry brine" the chicken. Start by salting the entire surface of the poultry with salt and your additional seasonings. Get salt both on top and underneath the skin of the bird and allow the bird to sit uncovered in the refrigerator for four hours. Blot dry with paper towels completely before cooking. Similarly, some Asian techniques recommend "pre treating" the bird before refrigeration by pouring boiling salted water over the bird and then blotting the tacky skin dry.

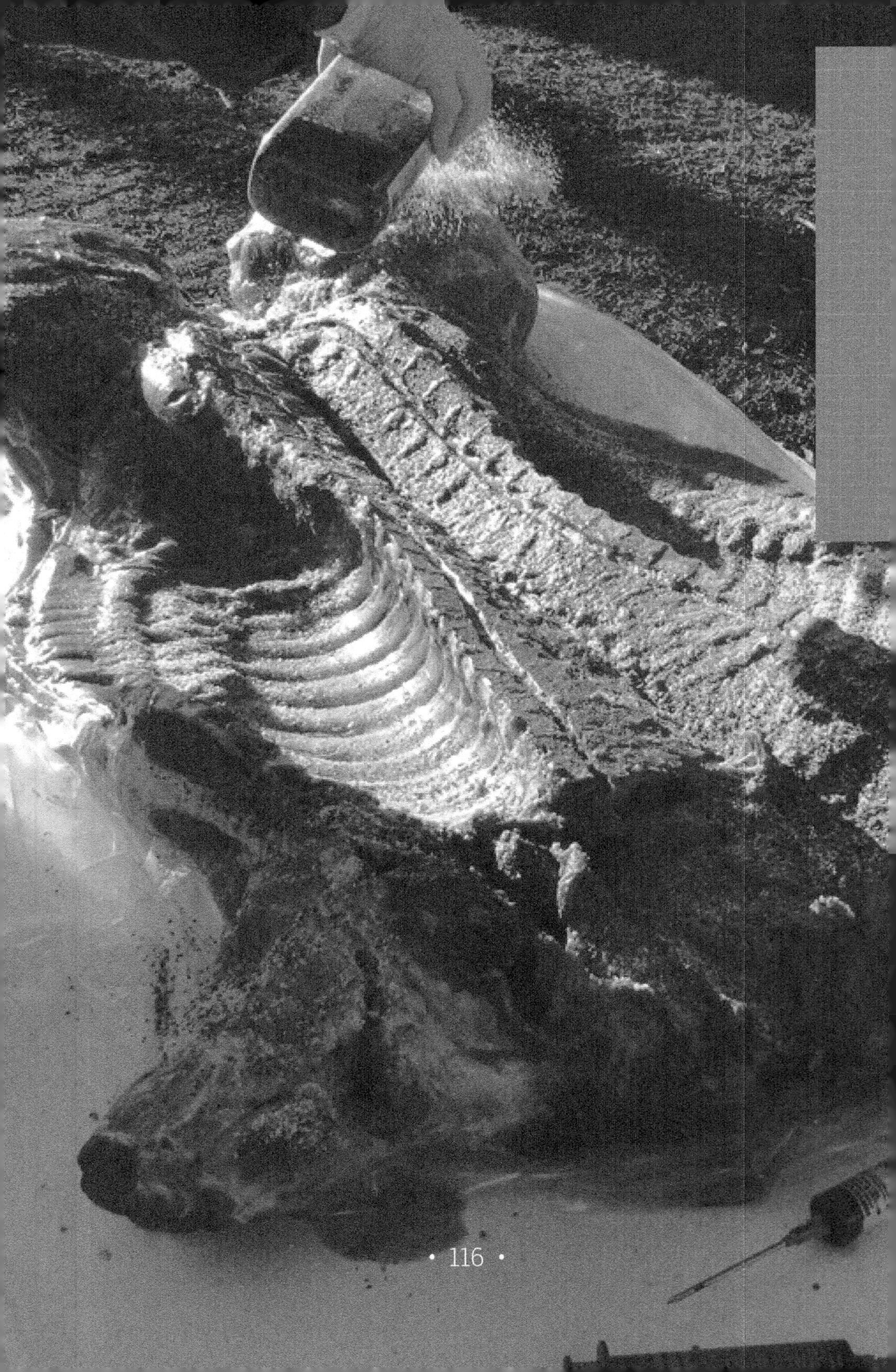

WHOLE HOG

Now, the Whole Hog is a lot of work. It's a specialty that's high in the BBQ hierarchy but also falls in the unusual category of being uncommon. Whole hog competitions are a dying breed. In the backyard, a whole hog is just usually too much and in restaurants only a few brave entrepeneur Pit masters are ready to create the infrastructure needed for whole Hog. We'll talk to one of the best in a minute. But first, there are three main things you'll need:

- A way to transport your pig.

- A way to keep your pig from getting warm (bathtub full of ice or giant coolers work).

- And finally a vessel large enough to cook it slowly.

Then there are the steps you'll want to follow when cooking your first whole hog.

1. First, you will want to source your hog. This is typically a visit to a real butcher (another dying breed) or the butcher in your local supermarket. If that fails, try a friend of a friend that runs a restaurant.

2. Decide how big. A 100-125 pound hog serves 80 to 100 people when cooked down. If you need more meat, consider adding a few butts or shoulders instead of trying two.

3. Decide if you want the head on or off, and if you want to avoid using power tools for dinner, you can request that it comes split with the spine pre-cut. This is cutting through heavy duty bone and is best left to a pro.

4. You'll still have trimming to do. Begin carving away any organs left attached (if any), next pull the spinal cord and discard (both sides), remove the membrane on the back side of the ribs and trim away any other visible sinew or silver skin. You'll want the skin to act as a

natural shield to catch drippings so don't trim away too much skin; however many Pit masters like to trim away some skin on the larger portions of the shoulders and ham portions (the inside tops of the crotch and armpits) to allow for the creation of more crusty bark formation.

5. Carolina Pit master founder, and three-time South Carolina State Hog Cooking Champion, Jack Waiboer's tip: At this point you can also carve out and discard a thick portion of the spine near the neck. This can potentially save almost an hour in cook time, and you are not wasting any prime meat.

6. Clean the entire hog inside and out with a hose and water (if the room allows) or by "sponge bath with clean cotton hand rags and a gallon of white vinegar.

7. Season the hog by first applying a slather of cheap yellow mustard across the entire surface of the inside meat of the hog. The mustard will act as an adherent for your favorite spice rub or Hog Rub

8. Inject the loins, hams, and shoulders with an injection of apple juice and cider vinegar. You'll probably want a fancy heavy duty injector thingy, but I've always been successful with the cheap plastic turkey injector syringes that are most common. Just keep the spices in your injection juice to a minimum to allow easy flow through whatever injector you use.

9. Smoke over indirect heat of 250°. You'll want to be cautious of any open flame beneath the hog as inevitable drippings (that can flow more as well as drip) can cause a fierce grease fire. Direct the ham (larger cuts) nearest the heat source.

10. A typical 100 lb. hog should take twelve to thirteen hours to cook. Add two hours or so for each additional 25 pounds. Cook until shoulders reach 196° and the hams reach an internal temperature of 185° - 195° F.

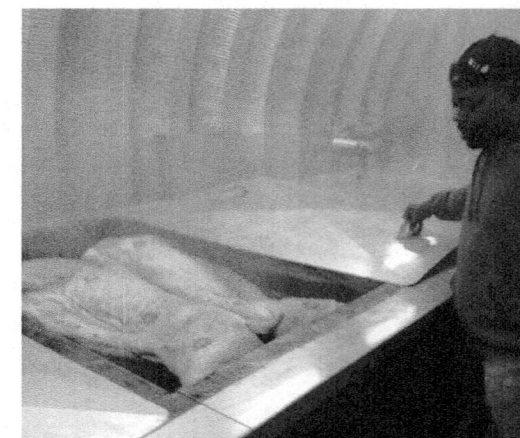

WHOLE HOG THE SCOTT'S BBQ WAY

I've come to learn there is one guy in the South East U.S. that is arguably the best hog cooker in the world. He just so happens to smoke about an hour's drive out my front door. I paid a visit on a cold February morning, and as we walked up, we couldn't help but notice the music was LOUD. Even from across the street-over and above the ventilation fan's hum - you could hear Clarence Carter's "Strokin'" thumpin'. The Scott's smokehouse is impressive too. One half utility barn and one half spaceship with aromatic hardwood smoke seeping slowly into every fiber of your clothes.

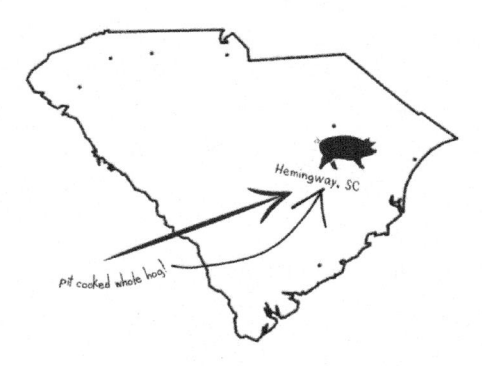

Inside was the Pit Master, Rodney Scott. After talking and eating I am convinced Hemingway, South Carolina has become the epicenter of the BBQ universe.

"This one's been on since yesterday afternoon around 5:30 or 6 o'clock. I have some other dry seasonings I use before I mop it - a little salt pepper - that kinda thing, then I mop it - just blend it all in," says Rodney.
Mmm mmm!

Bill West

I got right into the BBQ & A: "What keeps you going?" I asked.

"Meeting the new people - satisfying the customer with the good flavor... that's my favorite part...
Are we live right now? I don't tend to cuss...

I grew up in the business ... My dad started in 1972... And growing up working with my dad cutting wood - farming - That kind of thing. I saw that cooking hogs was a little easier than farming... Started to pay real close attention, and here we are...Back on it. Once I found out that food was in supply and demand, I said wow we can introduce this to anybody. My favorite part of it is meeting new people every week - Making new friends. Satisfying the appetite of the visitor."

Q: Do you have a secret recipe?

"I wouldn't say necessarily secret... As a good friend Nick Pihakis (Jim 'N Nick's) once said, "Food hasn't changed - people change the way they do food." To me, it's mostly technique, and our secret is WHEN we put whatever we put in the sauce and HOW LONG we cook with whatever."

"The key to making BBQ incredible in my opinion is love. You put a lot of love into it and a lot of time and effort, and you're pretty sure to get the same response back. It's not easy, but that's the main ingredient as far as I'm concerned - the hard work, the effort, and the love, for the whole thing."

Q: What Region of BBQ do you serve — South Carolina?

"I would consider myself pure southeastern South Carolina. Around here most guys do whole hog. But other places people do whole shoulders. I don't consider it rare; it's just that a lot of people don't want to go through the hard work of lifting an entire animal every day."

Q: What makes whole hog different?

"I have this thought that somehow the back bone flavors the entire animal, and when you cook a half a hog as opposed to a whole hog, it seems that the juices are kinda not staying within the entire animal; but when you have the entire animal - the backbone - belly - rib meat - shoulder meat, the juices all interact and give it that unique flavor.

When we put a portion on a plate, we like to have a little ham, a little belly, a little shoulder, and maybe a little loin. A little bit of everything so maybe you can get a touch of flavor from all parts of the hog. We keep it all together that's the way I was taught. It's pretty much the way we stick with the tradition of what was taught to us...what my dad taught me."

Q: What has this hog gone through already?

"So far this hog has only gone through roasting all night - slow smoke and we turn it over after twelve hours. At twelve hours when we turn it over, we put on our dry seasonings and salt and pepper, and then we mop it after that. All at the same time we have a little heat under it baking the skins while we're putting all the seasonings on it at the same time."

Q: Where does it go after the pit?

"From here we'll take it and add a little bit more seasoning, and then we'll pull it all by hand, put it in pans, portion it up and serve it. That's why we like to get it tender, moist and juicy so you can just grab it and pull it apart with no problem."

Q: What are you looking for in the end - texture?

There's a little texture in the end on the meat that we watch for. As far as seasonings we want all to have seasoning and sauce - covered and flavored.

On the bottom, the skin should crisp up. Once we got all that nice and crispy, we'll cut that up and sell it as well."

Q: How many can you cook here?

"I can do twenty hogs inside the entire building. We have single pits on this side (gesturing). Six right here, two doubles down here, four there, and that entire side holds doubles, which is ten, so we have double pits for even numbers and say if we have to cook nine hogs, we got single pits that can accommodate a single as well.

This mop sauce is black pepper, red pepper, vinegar and a whole lotta love. And lemons – a little citrus flavor in there. A little sweetness in there, but not so much that you have to go to the local dentist when you're done. We go through about eight to ten gallons a day with extra sauces and mopping the hogs. Some people call it Mop Sauce some people call it mop. Depends on where you're from I guess. This is what we will call sauce here at Scott's barbecue. The same thing you're getting at the table.

Different sauce categories I've heard of have been vinegar based, pepper, tomato, molasses and of course mustard, but the only thing we've known here in this area is vinegar based. Eastern Carolina. From Columbia - the midlands west - everybody is considered to use mostly mustard based sauces. I like the vinegar the best."

Q: Do you break apart the ribs and all while you're mopping and basting?

"I like to break it up to make sure all the whole hog is covered with sauce. All the juices get through. So while you're baking the skins, all the flavor is still trapped right in and everything is getting seasoned, so when you pull it you have everything you need."

Q: What's a typical day for you here?

"Typical day - I wake up, get dressed, get some breakfast and come to work and I'll flip my hog over because they've roasted all night. I'll have my guys here all night, and I start seasoning. The first two hogs come off around opening - 9:30, and I'll have some more coming off around noon. And the last batch will probably come off around three so that we'll have whole hogs hot all day. So we'll stage them out to make sure the meat stays hot and moist all day long.

In the middle of the night, there's a lot of story telling! The hogs are cooking slow. They go on evening time around four or five o'clock. We get a delivery, we get 'Econ and we start slow roasting them from then on until the next day. The process never stops. We light the fire on Tuesday nights for Wednesday service and the fire burns from Tuesday until Saturday night."

Q: Tell me about this new smokehouse.

"The original one burned down couple of years ago. This one was designed by a good friend of mine, Reggie Gibson. He designed this one to be windproof noncombustible - the main thing we needed - something that wouldn't burn and pretty much all natural with skylights. Simple building, but very functional. Kinda looks like a spaceship. This was built back in August 2015. I want to think all Pit masters have a fire at some point. It's not good, but it happens."

Q: What would surprise people about this place?

"A lot of people don't realize just how long it takes to cook a hog, but it's pretty much a half a days work.They're surprised that it takes so long to cook a hog and the way we do it - the last few minutes is only thirty minutes of work and then it's done."

Q: What keeps you going everyday?

"Music, man! Music motivation. And that new person that shows up and wants to see what we got and hopefully we satisfy them.

Man, my playlist is everything from Chitlin' Circuit to R&B to Country, a little Jazz, most of the time it's a lot of R&B, Jazz and old school hip hop - you know upbeat music."
Favorite tracks? "Best of Me by Anthony Hamilton is one of my favorites, Don't make Me Beg by Tucker, OPP - Naughty by Nature, it goes all over!"

HOG RUB

Use a cheap yellow mustard (no Gray Poupon here) to adhere this coarse spice blend to the exposed pork (not skin).

- 3 cups garlic pepper blend
- 3 cups kosher salt
- 1 cup brown sugar
- 1 cup paprika

Mix all the ingredients. Make ahead of time and store in a cool dark place.

HOG INJECTION

Take your time injecting this sweet brine into every crevice of the pork. The flesh should plump up and be noticibly larger and heavier when you are done.

- 2 ½ cups Apple juice
- 1 cup Apple cider vinegar

- 1 cup water
- 1 cup brown sugar
- 4 Tbsp kosher salt
- 4 Tbsp quality Worcestershire sauce

Mix all the ingredients and dissolve completely. Use syringe style injector probed into the thickest parts of the meat.

COOKS LOG

There are many variables in the perfect barbecue. Time of day. Wind and weather. Type of fuel. One trick as you get more serious in your grilling and smoking endeavors is to keep a log and an ongoing notebook of your cooks. Trial and error should be noted and victories recorded to try again. Even if you are not competing, a log like the one that follows can come in handy for mastering the backyard cook and perfecting different cooker characteristics. Also available at:http://barbecuetricks.com/book-resources

BBQ Cook Log

Event _____ Date(s): _____

Meat Type [_____] Brand/Style/Cut [_____] Fresh _____

Weight [_____] Price / lb [_____] Frozen _____

Pit [_____] Pit Location [_____] # of Pieces [_____]

Preparation _____
Procedure _____
Used _____
_____
_____
_____

Rubs _____ Mops _____
Seasonings _____ Glazes _____
Marinades _____ Sauces _____

Post Prep Rest Time [_____] Marinade/Brine Time [_____]

Cooking _____
Procedure _____
Used _____

Target Cooker Temp [_____] Actual Temp [_____] Smoking Time [_____] Final Internal Meat Temp [_____]

Time in [_____] Time out [_____] Total Time [_____]

Fuel Type/Brand Qty Used [_____] [_____] [_____] Smoke Wood Qty Used [_____] [_____] Dry _____
Soaked _____

Comments _____
Before _____
Cooking _____

Weather Conditions _____

Bill West • 127

Chapter 6

Finishing
TOUCHES
(SAUCES)

" Barbecue sauce is like a beautiful woman.
If it's too sweet it's bound to be hiding something. "

– Lyle Lovett

Chapter 6

I call this chapter the finishing touch because I usually use sauces at the end of the grilling process. A few sauce rules:

- The sweeter the sauce the later you want to add it in. Sugary sauces will burn quickly. That little bit of char may also be the extra flavor and texture punch you're looking for.

- Some sauces are deemed "finishing sauces" because they are indeed reserved for the end of the cook.

- A mop sauce (sometimes just called a mop) is a thin sauce that is typically light on sugar that a pit master will use several times throughout the entire cook. The mop will add layers of flavor while also continuing to keep the meat moist.

- Avoid recycling a marinade as a sauce. Once the liquid has made contact with meat it can become a playground for bacteria unless it is brought to a boil.

SOUTH CAROLINA MUSTARD BASED SAUCE

I make my home in South Carolina. The Palmetto state is home to a different kind of barbecue sauce. As discussed in chapter one, our Northern brethren in Western North Carolina have staked their claim in a vinegary thin and spicy sauce that cuts the fattiness of whole hog pulled pork. But here in South Carolinia, we like to keep our options open. South Carolina is, in fact, the only place you can find a mustard based style of barbecue sauce.

The origins of the mustard infusion is said to have been passed down from German influences from settlers on the Carolina coast. In the mid 1700s the British Colony of South Carolina brought in thousands of families to the area to settle in and make the area their home. The settlers brought with them traditional German fair. With it came a common use of mustard. To this day most of the biggest names in South Carolina are of German decent including the Bessinger family who still wave the mustard flag (called Carolina Gold) in their BBQ joints in the Columbia and Charleston area.

Although the thought of a mustard sauce is foreign to many. Barbecue fans tend to like this tangy take on a thick sweet sauce. There are hundreds of variations that can be created with different varieties of mustard (almost like cheese and wine) but tradition leans to a simple, affordable, yellow blend that we've adapted below. This mainstream slurry of mustard and vinegar makes for another tangy way to cut through fatty pulled pork at your next pig pickin'.

»

SOUTH CAROLINA MUSTARD SAUCE

Also known as "Carolina Gold" this tangy and sweet sauce uses basic yellow mustard as the key ingredient. Serve this sauce warm, on the side, with pulled pork or mix below amount directly with one shredded/pulled Boston butt.

- **1 small white onion, minced**
- **2 Tbsp butter**
- **1 clove of garlic, minced**
- **1 cup yellow mustard**
- **¾ cup brown sugar**
- **¾ cup pickle juice or cider vinegar**
- **1 tsp kosher salt**
- **1 tsp fresh ground black pepper**
- **Hot sauce to taste**

Instructions:

Saute garlic and onion until translucent. Add mustard and remaining ingredients and simmer for ten minutes until thickened. Strain out onion pulp (optional).

NORTH CAROLINA VINEGAR SAUCE

North and South Carolina are indeed different entities. One difference is in sauce appeal. Cross the state line and things get a lot more sour in the the form of Western Carolina Vinegar sauce. Tart, hot, a li'l bit sweet, but thin enough to mix quietly into a pile of pulled pork without getting in the way of the smoke in the meat.

- **1 cup cider vinegar**
- **½ cup ketchup**
- **1 Tbsp crushed red pepper**
- **½ tsp black pepper (secret: McCormick's Worcestershire flavored)**
- **1 tsp kosher salt**
- **½ tsp ground mustard**
- **½ tsp celery salt**
- **1 tsp plum sauce (or dark molasses)**
- **1 tsp brown sugar**
- **1 tsp Worcestershire sauce**

Use an empty 16oz bottle (from cider vinegar or the like) for this sauce to store and serve. Simmer ingredients in a small to medium sauce pan for ten minutes. Let cool before serving.

Bill West • 135

ALABAMA WHITE SAUCE

Big Bob Gibson's is a big name in BBQ, especially when it comes to this white sauce.... An Alabama Barbecue tradition, it uses mayonnaise at its core, and Bob Gibson of Decatur, Alabama, is the guy whom they say launched it way back in the 1920's. You'll want to apply this only at the very end of your grilling or smoking. It will breakdown and separate if it is heated too long. It's tangy and thinner than you might think — when grilling chicken; brush lightly over the chicken during the last few minutes of grilling.

- **¾ cup mayonnaise**
- **1/3 cup apple cider vinegar**
- **¼ cup lemon juice**
- **¼ cup apple juice (I used corn syrup here)**
- **1 Tbsp granulated garlic**
- **1 Tbsp prepared horseradish**
- **1 Tbsp coarsely ground black pepper**
- **1 tsp mustard powder**
- **¼ tsp salt**
- **½ tsp finely ground Cayenne pepper**

Place all ingredients in a very large blender or food processor. Blend for one minute, or until thoroughly mixed and sauce is smooth. We used a bullet blender. Remember it's almost like a mop — use it to slather on in the very end of the cooking process. You may first want to try it as a dip. Mainly for chicken.

BLUE SAUCE

This blueberry based sauce is unlike anything you've tried before. This version uses dried blueberries simply because we couldn't find fresh berries (out of season) at the time of this writing. Don't expect a Smurf blue color... and that's probably a good thing. The color is subtle (often hard to detect) but the blueberry is defiantly in the flavor. Perfect for beef or chicken. Maybe a side of blue potatoes? The added bonus is it's a great conversation starter.

- **2 cups water**
- **½ cup ketchup**
- **½ cup dried blueberries, minced**
- **1 Tbsp balsamic vinegar**
- **1 Tbsp Worcestershire sauce**
- **1 tsp Sriracha**
- **1 tsp liquid smoke**
- **1 tsp Dijon mustard**
- **Salt and pepper**

Add water, blueberries and vinegar to sauce pan and simmer for five to ten minutes. Add remaining ingredients and simmer on low heat until desired thickness. Season to taste with salt and pepper. Strain out blueberry pulp using spoon to force out additional liquid. Discard MOST pulp. If you want to try a fresh blueberry version head to blueberrycouncil.org Try it with 1-2 cups fresh (or frozen blueberries) pulsed in a blender first. Team this Blue sauce with any traditional ketchup based (red) sauce, and the unique Alabama White sauce, and you've got a Red, White & Blue patriotic BBQ!

COCA COLA SAUCE

Some BBQ sauce mixologists have a secret ingredient they'll never reveal. In this BBQ sauce recipe, the secret ingredient isn't very secret. The trick is right there in the name. Coca Cola is the secret ingredient in the Coca Cola BBQ sauce, and it's super easy to make.

This sauce is a great addition to an everyday cook out. The distinct cola flavor actually fades away in the mixing and simmering so your guests will be left wondering what the secret ingedient is...

Feel free to experiment with your beverage of choice. Root Beer and regional favorites like Cheerwine are common choices. In fact, the Dr. Pepper Company actually mass produces a **Dr. Pepper BBQ Sauce**.

The 90 minute to two hour simmer will allow this sauce to thicken as much as you like, and as most sauces do, it will thicken more when cool.

- **2 cans Coca-Cola (12 oz each)**
- **1 ½ cups ketchup**
- **½ cup cider vinegar**
- **½ onion, minced**
- **1 ½ Tbsp black pepper**
- **¼ cup brown sugar**
- **3 Tbsp salt**
- **1 and ½ Tbsp chili powder**

Combine ingredients in medium saucepan and simmer for one to two hours or until desired thickness. For a less chunky sauce, strain out remaining minced onions.

TEXAS MOP SAUCE

When barbecuing big slabs of **beef like Brisket** or Tri-Tip, the Texans know a secret trick. Slather on the sauce early and often throughout the low and slow cooking process to layer on Texas sized flavor.

In fact, the unique sauce they use inherited a new name and BBQ classification. The thin sauce is called a "Mop" because it's typically too thin to hold on to a regular basting brush and requires a "mop" type floppy cotton yarn brush to soak up the liquid and baste over the meat. It's a sloppy process.

History has it that President Johnson's barbecue master Walter Jetton (yep, he had a BBQ master) made the mop famous in his 1960's era book.

When used in Texas sized PITS sometimes a real household mop is re-purposed for this task to handle the huge quantity. More likely you'll want to use a normal sized brisket and a commercially available "drawer sized" bbq mop like the one shown (or this **Sauce Mop and Bucket Set** from Amazon).

Use this peppery coffee mop sauce liberally on large cuts of beef to layer on flavor and keep the moisture in the meat. Over time, the mop will facilitate a rustic sweet bark on the surface of the meat.

- **1 cup dark/strong coffee**
- **1 Tbsp sugar**
- **1 cup ketchup**
- **1 full Tbsp fresh coarse ground black pepper**
- **1 Tbsp kosher salt**
- **¼ cup butter**
- **½ cup Worcestershire sauce**

Mix ingredients in large pot or sauce pan with enough room to place mop without overflow. Simmer lightly for 20 minutes. Mop (sauce) should be used thin to baste meat. Allow to thicken for a spicy "sop" to serve plate-side.

DANNY'S GLAZE FOR PORK

I first heard of Danny Gaulden's Glaze when shooting a GrateTV episode on **Twice Smoked Ham with Jack Waiboer.** He used this glaze on other occasions too and said it was the best around. After researching the best glaze recipe to share, Gaulden's name kept coming up. It's interesting to note that I found several variations on this same recipe!

So I went to the source...http://dannysbbq.com where Gaulden actually has a 2003 update on his original 1999 version (the original had a beer option instead of the vinegar). Jack Waiboer suggests a bit of Southern Comfort in lieu of some vinegar. Meathead at **Amazing Ribs** suggests "amping" it up with some hot sauce.

The basic 4 parts brown sugar, 1 part mustard, and 1 part cider vinegar seems just right to me. Gaulden suggests using it on ribs IMMEDIATELY after pulling them off the grill. Check out **his site** and give his recipes a try.

- **1 cup brown sugar**
- **¼ cup yellow mustard**
- **¼ cup cider vinegar**

Instructions: Mix together ingredients cool. Then simmer. Baste ribs immediately after pulling off the grill. It's perfect for pork, like a ham glaze, ribs and also good on beef.

KANSAS CITY SAUCE

Some folks consider Kansas City the epicenter of American BBQ. Fans of South Carolina Mustard sauce, Carolina Vinegar Sauce, and Texas Sauce would surely beg to differ. KC has a good argument. Kansas City BBQ Sauce is one of the most popular off the shelf sauces in grocery stores, and the Kansas City Barbecue Society is the largest and most influential sanctioning organizations in existence.

Mainstream America loves a super sweet smokey thick sauce, and that's exactly what Kansas City, MO specializes in. The style of sauce has been commercialized under the brand KC Masterpiece. A child psychologist, Rich Davis, developed the recipe in 1977 originally with only five ingredients. Since then it was purchased by Kingsford and has become one of the top selling barbecue sauces in the nation.

Our version of Kansas City sauce has that same deep rich tomato undertone with a sweet smokey finish. It's the perfect sauce for both chicken and pork as it literally defines the phrase "sticks to your ribs."

- **1 fifteen oz can crushed tomato**
- **½ cup dark corn syrup**
- **2 Tbsp butter**
- **¼ cup brown sugar**
- **½ cup white vinegar**
- **1 Tbsp chili powder**
- **1 tsp liquid smoke**
- **1 tsp garlic powder**
- **1 tsp onion powder**
- **½ tsp ground celery seed**
- **½ tsp salt**
- **½ tsp pepper**
- **½ tsp cinnamon**

Add the butter to a small non-reactive saucepan and melt. Add vinegar and remaining ingredients and stir until blended. Simmer over low heat for 20 minutes. Clean the stove.

This tomatoey sweet and thick sauce is a mainstream American favorite for ribs, sliced pork, and chicken. Oh yeah, you'll need to serve extra on the side.

CHINESE BBQ SAUCE

There's something exotic about a good Hoisin Sauce. It's hard to tell what ingredients make it so unique. The soybeans? Garlic? Plums? It's the Chinese ketchup, and it's the starting point to making our US knock-off Chinese BBQ Sauce.

The fresh ingredients make this sauce really zippy. I mean if you put fresh garlic, Hoisin, and fresh ginger in my Elmer's Glue I would probably eat it... but in this blend of fresh sweet and tangy ingredients, it'll make you want to eat it like soup. But save some for everybody.

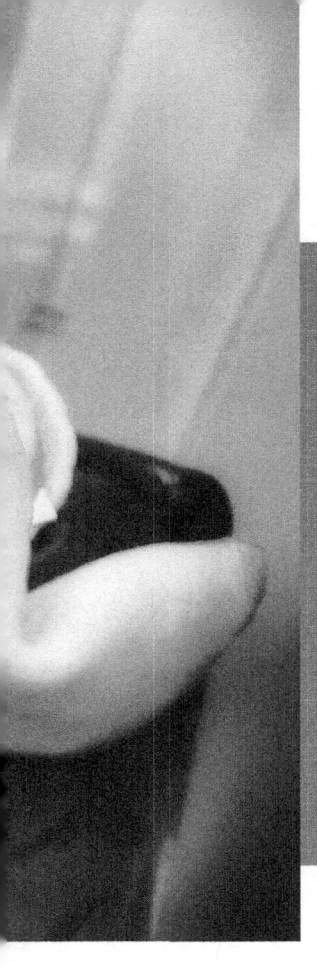

This Chinese BBQ Sauce recipe is especially good on chicken and nice and sticky for spare ribs - Fortune cookie optional.

- ¼ cup hoisin sauce
- 2 Tbsp dry sherry
- 2 Tbsp soy sauce
- 2 Tbsp sugar
- 1 Tbsp fresh grated ginger
- 5 Tbsp ketchup
- 2 Tbsp rice vinegar
- 3 small cloves of minced garlic (pressed in garlic press)
- 1 tsp sesame oil
- 1 finely minced green onion

This American version of a Chinese BBQ sauce has a freshness you can't get in bottled brands that comes from the sherry, fresh ginger, and garlic. It's perfect to give an average backyard cookout a bit of an international flair.

Combine all ingredients except oil and simmer for five minutes. Add sesame oil at end. Stir and serve.

For a dynamic dipping sauce add 1 ½ Tbsp of smooth peanut butter.

WHAT'S THIS HERE SAUCE

This Worcestershire (what's this here?) based sweet and tangy red barbecue sauce is my favorite of all the sauces. Serve it hot on the side or slather it on wings or any meat at the end of the grilling process to add a superior glaze and tasty char.

- 2 Tbsp vegetable oil
- 1 large clove of garlic, minced
- 1 medium onion, minced
- 1 Chipotle pepper, minced
- 1 tsp chili powder
- ¼ tsp Cayenne pepper
- 1 cup ketchup
- 2 Tbsp Dijon Mustard (Grey Poupon)
- 5 Tbsp dark molasses
- 3 Tbsp Worcestershire sauce
- ½ tsp fresh ground black pepper
- 2 tsp Texas Pete

The best thing about this sauce is that it's a perfect sweet heat finishing sauce that will caramelize perfectly as the final touch to ribs and chicken. Feel free to temper the heat by dropping the cayenne or chipotle.

Heat the oil in a deep sauce pan and add garlic and onions until they soften. Add all peppers and heat for 20 seconds before stirring in the remaining ingredients. Cook on low heat for 20 minutes until thickened. When cool, strain out onion and garlic "chunks" if desired. It's a hit with pork, chicken, and beef. Yields 5 Servings

JACK D'S HONEY MUSTARD

Would you like your booze on ice or on your meat? Yes, please. This Jack Daniel's infused gold sauce gives new meaning to the term "get sauced."

- ½ cup honey
- ½ cup cider vinegar
- ½ cup dark brown sugar, packed
- 2 eggs
- 2 Tbsp flour
- 2 Tbsp prepared French's yellow mustard
- ½ cup Jack Daniel's whiskey
- 9 oz bottle Kraft's horseradish (cream)

Mix honey, vinegar, sugar, eggs and flour in a blender and pulse a few seconds to mix at high speed until smooth. Combine ingredients in a medium saucepan and simmer until desired thickness. Continue to stir and whisk briskly to avoid any sticking to the bottom of the saucepan. It will thicken just as it comes to a boil. Then promptly add whiskey and mustard. After thirty more seconds stirring and cooking remove from heat. Add the horseradish and mix thoroughly. Allow to cool completely before serving or storing.

JACK DANIEL'S MARINADE

Would you like to soak in your booze? Alrighty then! This Tennessee whiskey infused marinade is just the thing.

- ¼ cup Jack Daniel's whiskey
- ¼ cup soy sauce
- ¼ cup Dijon-style mustard
- ¼ cup minced green onion and tops
- **Pepper to taste**
- ¼ cup firmly packed light brown sugar
- **1 tsp salt**
- **Dash of Worcestershire sauce**

Combine all ingredients in a non reactive bowl or plastic Tupperware style marinating container. Marinate seafood and shrimp for an hour in refrigerator. Beef and chicken can be marinated four hours or longer. Reserve one cup before marinating for a brush-on basting sauce.

IMPOSTER A-1 STEAK SAUCE

Sure you can buy it for ten bucks less than it will cost you to make this at home. But who doesn't like a challenge?

- ½ cup orange juice
- ½ cup raisins
- ¼ cup soy sauce
- ¼ cup white vinegar
- 2 Tbsp Dijon mustard
- 1 Tbsp bottled grated orange peel
- 2 Tbsp Heinz Ketchup
- 2 Tbsp Heinz Chili Sauce

Combine all ingredients in a medium saucepan and bring ingrdients to a boil for two to three minutes stirring continuously. Allow to cool off the heat until just warm. Blend and puree in food processor or "magic bullet" type blender until smooth. Seal and refrigerate for up to 90 days until used.

LAWRY'S-LIKE SEASONED SALT

My favorite spice on French fries is Lawry's. Thanks to the interwebs we've cracked the secret code:

- 2 Tbsp pepper
- 1 Tbsp chicken bouillon powder
- 1 tsp onion salt
- 1 tsp onion powder
- 1 Tbsp garlic salt
- 1 tsp cumin powder
- 1 tsp dry marjoram leaves
- 1 Tbsp minced parsley
- 1 tsp paprika
- ½ tsp curry powder
- 1 Tbsp chili powder
- 1/3 cup salt

Combine ingredients in a bowl using a fork, wisk, or your fingers to mix and remove/blend in any clumps. Store in air tight container or mason jar. Keep at room temperature. Use within 3 months. Makes about 1 cup.

KENNY ROGER'S BBQ SAUCE

My favorite Kenny Roger's song has got to be "The Greatest," a single he played for me live on the air while visiting my radio station in Savannah, Georgia. He's always been great to his fans, and I've since found out that he also liked to cook. Kenny and the former Governor of Kentucky (and KFC developer) John Brown started the Kenny Rogers Roasters chain in 1991. I was surprised to see that, according to their website as of this writing, there are still a few franchised stores mainly in Singapore and Asia. Although I never had a chance to visit one of his "roasted" chicken joints I was able to dig up a facimile of his beloved barbecue sauce.

- **1 cup applesauce**
- **½ cup Heinz Ketchup**
- **1 ¼ cups light brown sugar, packed**
- **6 Tbsp lemon juice**
- **Salt and pepper**
- **½ tsp paprika**
- **½ tsp garlic salt**
- **½ tsp cinnamon**

Combine ingredients in a medium saucepan and simmer for fifteen minutes on low until desired thickness and fully dissolved. Serve cool or warmed in double boiler basted on meat.

(COME 'N GIT IT) OLD BAY SEASONING

There's nothing like the flavor of seafood spiked with a pinch of Old Bay. Originally named after the Old Bay Line, a passenger ship in the Chesepeake Bay back in the early 1900s, it has come to be a signature flavor for crab and shrimp for the McCormick spice company in an iconic blue and yellow can.

- **1 Tbsp celery seed**
- **1 Tbsp whole black peppercorns**
- **6 bay leaves**
- **½ tsp whole cardamom**
- **½ tsp mustard seed**
- **4 whole cloves**
- **1 tsp sweet hungarian paprika**
- **¼ tsp mace**
- **Dash of salt**

To boost flavors toast ingredients briefly in a dry pan for a few seconds to bloom and activate natual oils in the spices. Grind in a spice grinder, food processor, magic bullet, or even a coffee grinder. Combine ingredients in a bowl using a fork, wisk, or your fingers to mix and remove/blend in any clumps. Store in air tight container or mason jar. Keep at room temperature. Use within 3 months. Makes about 1 cup.

PAUL'S CAJUN SEASONING

Mix carefully as this Cajun spice has been known to make a chef or two launch into a fit of sneezing thanks to the sneezing powder one-two punch of cayenne and white pepper.

- **1 Tbsp paprika**
- **2 ½ tsp salt**
- **1 tsp onion powder**
- **1 tsp garlic powder**
- **1 tsp ground red pepper (cayenne)**
- **¾ tsp white pepper**
- **¾ tsp black pepper**
- **½ tsp dried thyme leaves**
- **½ tsp dried oregano leaves**

Combine ingredients well in a bowl using a fork, whisk, or your fingers to mix and remove/blend in any clumps. Store in air tight container or mason jar. Store in the dark at room temperature. Use within 3 months. Makes about 1 cup.

OUTBACK MARINADE

Outback Steakhouse is one of the most popular steakhouses. They have a great reputation for using quality aged beef and cooking over oak wood.

- **1 cup Scottish (or similar) ale**
- **2 tsp brown sugar**
- **½ tsp McCormick's seasoned salt**
- **¼ tsp ground black pepper**
- **¼ tsp MSG**

Marinate your favorite steak cut in beer only, for one hour in the refrigerator. Mix remaining dry ingredients, remove steak from beer marinade, and rub both sides with dry spice mixture. Allow to set and marinate for an additional 30 minutes in refrigerator before cooking.

Bill West

TMI FRIDAY'S GLAZE

They probably think this secret glaze recipe is "TMI." But if you look forward to TGI Friday's Whiskey Glaze, here's a way to recreate the super sweet finishing sauce at home. Wait until the end of your grilling to brush on meat to keep the sugar from burning.

- **1 head of garlic**
- **1 Tbsp olive oil**
- **⅔ cup water**
- **1 cup pineapple juice**
- **¼ cup teriyaki sauce**
- **1 Tbsp soy sauce**
- **1 1/3 cups dark brown sugar**
- **3 Tbsp lemon juice**
- **3 Tbsp minced white onion**
- **1 Tbsp Jack Daniels Whiskey**
- **1 Tbsp crushed pineapple**
- **¼ tsp cayenne pepper**

Remove excessive papery skin from garlic and slice small layer off the top. Coat the head of garlic with olive oil and roast in a 325° oven for up to thirty minutes or until soft. Allow to cool.

Combine water, pineapple juice, teriyaki sauce, soy sauce, and brown sugar in a medium saucepan over medium/high heat. Stir occasionally until mixture boils then reduce heat until mixture is just simmering. Pinch and squeeze the head of garlic until the soft paste of the roasted garlic is extracted and throw away remaining skins. Blend and whisk to combine adding the rest of the ingredients. Simmer (being careful to control the boil) for 45 minutes allowing the sauce to reduce to a thick syrup.

TIGER SAUCE

This sweet and spicy hot sauce with the fierce tiger on the label is a treat on meat and barbecue, but it can get pricey for a very small bottle. If you're a heavy user, you can use this copy cat recipe and make an affordable gallon and sauce yourself silly.

- 1 (pint jar) pickled hot peppers
- 1 (29 oz can) tomato puree (with basil or other spices)
- 1 (6 oz) tomato sauce
- ½ (quart bottle) red wine vinegar
- 1 (6 oz bottle) Louisiana Hot Sauce (3 oz for milder sauce)
- ½ tsp garlic power
- 1 Tbsp MSG (Accent)
- 4 Tbsp red pepper flakes (2 Tbsp for milder sauce)
- ½ (18 oz) bottle hickory flavored barbecue sauce

Blend jalepenos and juice in a blender or food processor until smooth (removing stems if necessary). In a large non reactive bowl wisk the remaining ingredients together. Makes about a gallon. Store and refrigerate in squirt/picnic bottles.

WORCESTERSHIRE SAUCE

The secret flavor in Lea and Perrin's Worcestershire Sauce surprisingly comes from anchovies. It's one reason that it is hard to find a generic or any alterative brand that tastes nearly as good. If you can source quality anchovy fillets and have the time, you can make a hand crafted batch in your own kitchen. It's almost as easy as spelling the word Worcestershire.

- 1 Tbsp olive oil
- 6 oz peeled fresh horseradish, chopped
- 2 medium white onions, chopped
- 3 Tbsp minced jalapeno pepper
- 3 Tbsp minced garlic
- 1 Tsp coarsely ground black pepper
- 2 cups water
- 4 cup distilled white vinegar
- 1 cup molasses
- 2 cups dark corn syrup
- 1 oz chopped anchovy fillets, drained
- 12 whole cloves
- 1 Tbsp Salt
- 1 lemon; peeled

Heat the oil in a medium sauce pan and add aromatics and saute' for about five minutes or until they turn translucent. Add the rest of the ingredients and bring all to a boil briefly. Then reduce heat and simmer for one hour.

Strain with a collander or with thick cheesecloth and store in refrigerator. Best when aged over thirty days.

Bill West

�
BBQ Pantry essentials:

Chapter 7

SECRET INGREDIENTS and PANTRY ESSENTIALS

*" I cook with wine.
Sometimes I even add it to the food. "*

— W.C. Fields

Chapter 7

There is an infinite combination of spices, herbs, and flavors that combine to create the taste of barbecue. Rodney Scott of Scott's BBQ in Hemingway, South Carolina says that often times is the methods and cook times that comprise the "secret." None the less there are really only a handful of ingredients that can be considered "pantry essentials" for barbecue.

Herbs and spices make up the bulk of this list. What's the difference?

- Herbs grow. They're leafy (not woody) and in cooking they don't really like heat. Add herbs at the end.
- Spices "like" heat. Typically spices are bark, seeds, roots, and buds.

When it comes to cooking meat over live fire, I would consider "bone" as a secret ingredient. Albeit not one easily stored in the pantry.

I've paraphrased that old saying: "Beauty is skin deep... but FLAVOR is to the bone."

Sure you can save buying by the pound if you butcher out the bone but be careful that you're not cutting out potential flavor. There's an undocumented layer of flavor that many say is added when you cook BONE in. Rodney Scott's secret is to keep in ALL the bones. He insists there is a difference in flavor even when you cook half hogs vs. whole hog. He points out the spine (and all it's surface area) adds it's own secret flavor.

PANTRY ESSENTIALS

- All Spice – This is the key to jerk seasoning. AKA The pimento berry
- Black Pepper – Always grind to order
- Cajun Seasoning
- Cayenne Pepper
- Chili Powder – Make your own for the best flavor. Recipe in Chapter 4.
- Coffee – The new microground instant coffees are great in rubs.
- Corriander – AKA cilantro seed. See Rendezvous Ribs in Chapter 5
- Crushed Red pepper – A little bit goes a long way, but it kicks up flavor.
- Cumin
- Dry Mustard
- Garlic Powder
- Ginger
- Sweet and Smoked Paprika
- Morton's Tender Quick - AKA Fab is a curing salt (enhances smoke ring)
- Turbinado Sugar – AKA Sugar In The Raw (see below)
- Tamarind Concentrate
- Onion – Onions make me cry whenever my wife pays triple to buy "pre-chopped" at the grocery.

Sugar has already been mentioned a bunch in this book. We noted in competition BBQ "Judges like sweet." It's worth noting that all sugar is not created equal (no pun intended). White refined sugar is often replaced by brown sugar in many rubs and sauces for a deeper flavor, but Turbinado sugar (AKA Sugar In The Raw) is preferred by pitmasters because it is a less processed form of crystalized sugar that stands up to heat better than other forms of sugar. Plus its larger crystals add a welcome texture to robust rubs.

Sugars and sweet sauces are best added at the end of high heat grilling. Smoking temperatures shouldn't burn sugars, but use caution. The burning point (called scorch point) of sugar is just above 330°F / 165°C.

SMOKE POINTS OF FATS AND OILS

- Safflower Oil 510°F/265°C
- Beef Tallow 400°F/205°C
- Canola Oil 400°F/205°C
- Coconut 350°F/175°C
- Butter 250°F/ 150°C
- Butter (Clarified) 400°F/250°C
- Lard 370°F/185°C
- Chicken Fat (schmaltz) 375°F/190°C
- Grapeseed Oil 390°F/195°C
- Olive Oil (Extra Virgin) 320°F/160°C

Chapter 8

Difficult
DESSERTS

"The only time to eat diet food is when you're waiting for the steak to cook."

– Julia Child

Chapter 8

No giant meal of roasted meat is complete without a dessert that is equally as impressive. Here's a collection of our favorites that pair perfectly with a BBQ gathering and a few, like our spit rotisserie pineapple, that require the help of a live flame.

CLASSIC BANANA PUDDING

Banana pudding is NOT always created equal. Some people just have it down. This is THE BEST banana pudding you'll eat. It isn't that deep yellow color, it's practically white, because contrary to popular belief, you should use vanilla pudding, heavy cream and sweetened condensed milk, rather than imitation banana flavored pudding.

- **1 (14 oz) can sweetened condensed milk**
- **1 ½ cups cold water**
- **1 (4 oz) package instant vanilla pudding mix**
- **2 cups (1 pint) heavy cream, whipped**
- **36 vanilla wafers**
- **3 medium bananas, sliced and dipped in lemon juice**

Whisk sweetened condensed milk and water in large bowl.
Add pudding mix. Whisk 2 minutes or until well blended. Chill 5 minutes.
Fold in whipped cream.

SPOON 1 cup pudding mixture into 2 ½ quart glass serving bowl. Top with one-third each of the vanilla wafers, bananas, and remaining pudding. Repeat layering twice, ending with the pudding mixture.
CHILL thoroughly. If possible keep cold (as shown on opposite page) in pan or bowl of ice.

Garnish as desired. For individual serving pudding desserts, prepare mixture and layer in dessert dishes.
Makes 10 - 12 servings

ROTISSERIE PINEAPPLE

This recipe is simple. But you need a proper rotisserie you are comfortable with. The trick is to give the fruit some pizzazz with a nifty spiral cut.

- 2 Tbsp cocoa powder
- 1 large pineapple
- 1 stick of butter
- 1 cup cane sugar (Sugar in the Raw or Demerara Sugar)

Peel your pineapple with a sharp knife and create a spiral pattern to remove all the thorny "eyes" along the flesh of the fruit. These ridges not only look really cool they act as a receptacle for the butter, sugar, and cocoa "rub." Create "pilot hole" to help drive spit through core of the pineapple. Then skewer and secure with probes and pliers. Rub with reserved melted butter, cocoa, and sugar.

Spit roast over a drip pan for 30 to 40 minutes and then coat generously with warmed and combined sugar, butter, and cocoa mixture. Continue to spit roast and glaze until remaining paste is gone.

We used a crystal cane sugar because it has a higher burn temperature and it will create a caramel crust. Slice in rounds right off the spit or slice and serve with a dollop of ice cream. Your barbecue guests will think you are showing off and will love this flashy and delicious desert. Makes 7 servings

RED VELVET CAKE ROLLS

My wife said I couldn't finish this book without adding a chapter on desserts, and while we think all included here are fantastic, this one is to die for.

- ¼ cup powdered sugar
- 4 eggs, separated
- ½ cup plus 1/3 cup granulated sugar, divided
- 1 tsp vanilla extract
- 2 Tbsp (1 oz bottle) red food coloring
- ⅔ cup all-purpose flour
- ¼ cup cocoa
- ½ tsp baking powder
- ¼ tsp baking soda
- ⅛ tsp salt
- Powdered sugar to sprinkle on top
- 1 cup pecans, finely chopped

Cream cheese filling
- **8 oz cream cheese**
- **1 cup powdered sugar**
- **6 Tbsp soft butter**
- **1 tsp vanilla**

Heat oven to 375°. Line a jelly-roll pan with foil; generously grease foil. Sprinkle linen or thin cotton towel with ¼ cup powdered sugar. Beat egg whites in large bowl until soft peaks form; gradually add ½ cup granulated sugar, beating until stiff peaks form. Beat egg yolks and vanilla in medium bowl on medium speed of mixer 3 minutes. Gradually add remaining 1/3 cup granulated sugar; continue beating 2 additional minutes. Place red food color in liquid measuring cup; add water to make 1/3 cup. Stir together flour, cocoa, baking powder, baking soda, and salt. Add to egg yolk mixture alternately with colored water, beating on low speed just until batter is smooth. Gradually fold chocolate mixture into beaten egg whites until well blended. Spread batter evenly in prepared pan. Bake 12 to 15 minutes or until top springs back when touched lightly in center. Immediately loosen cake from edges of pan; invert onto prepared towel. Carefully peel off foil. Immediately roll cake and towel together starting from narrow end; place on wire rack to cool completely. Prepare cream cheese filling. Carefully unroll cake; remove towel. Spread filling over cake. Reroll cake without towel. Wrap filled cake with wax paper and wrap again with plastic wrap. Refrigerate with seam down at least 1 hour or until ready to serve. Just before serving, sprinkle top with additional powdered sugar. Drizzle with chocolate syrup and garnish with finely chopped pecans. Cover and keep refrigerated.

Cream cheese filling: Beat 1 package (8 oz) softened cream cheese, 1 cup powdered sugar, 6 tablespoons softened butter or margarine and 1 teaspoon vanilla extract in small mixer bowl until smooth. Makes 8 – 10 servings

We found this one a few years ago by accident. We were receiving a CSA box of fruits & veggies from a local farm and ended up with a TON of muscadines. Not having grown up in the south, I wasn't familiar with this grape, but I'm oh so familiar with this cake now...

- 2 ½ cups muscadines
- 1 box white cake mix
- 1 small box blackberry Jell-O
- ¾ cup oil
- 4 eggs
- 1 ¼ cup powdered sugar

Southern Muscadine Cake

Cook 2 ½ cups muscadines in 1 ½ cups water until hulls are tender (about 15 minutes). Place in a strainer/sieve on top of a bowl. Using a knife cut a slash in each one, and then mash to force juice and pulp through, leaving seeds and hulls. Separate hulls from seeds and discard seeds. Set hulls aside.

Mix one box white cake mix, one small box blackberry Jell-O, ¾ cup oil, 4 eggs and the muscadine juice/pulp, reserving 4 tablespoons. Beat until fluffy. Fold hulls into batter and pour into a greased and floured Bundt pan. Bake at 350° for about 45 minutes until done.

While baking, stir together powdered sugar with the reserved 4 tablespoons muscadine juice. Heat if necessary to blend. When cake is done, poke holes in the top and pour glaze over.

DEEP DISH PEACH COBBLER

I have learned deep dish is better than it's cousin...

- **2 sticks butter, melted**
- **2 cups milk**
- **2 cups sugar**
- **2 cups cake flour**
- **1 tsp vanilla**
- **2 cans of peaches, large**
- **2 9" deep dish pie shells, plus 2 regular 9" pie shells**
- **2 Tbsp melted butter, and 1 Tbsp sugar to sprinkle on top**

Combine first five ingredients. Stir in peaches and blend well. Pour into deep dish pie shells. Put the regular pie shells on top (trim). Brush with melted butter and sprinkle with sugar. Cut several slits in the top and bake at 350° for 35 minutes or until golden brown and bubbly. Cool and serve warm with vanilla ice cream. Makes two deep dish pies

GRANNY'S PERSIMMON PUDDING

I had never even heard of a persimmon (fruit) until Thanksgiving last year — really. Mix all ingredients thoroughly. Grease 2 round deep dish baking dishes and bake at 325° for 2 – 2 ½ hours until pudding turns dark.

- **2 eggs**
- **1 quart persimmons = 1 pint pulp (6 persimmons)**
- **2 ½ cups milk**
- **2 cups plain flour**
- **1 ⅔ cups sugar**
- **1 tsp salt**
- **1 tsp soda**
- **1 tsp baking powder**
- **½ tsp cinnamon**
- **¼ tsp vanilla**
- **4 Tbsp butter, melted**

Homemade Whipped Cream

- **2 cups heavy cream**
- **2 Tbsp sugar**
- **1 tsp vanilla**

Mix all ingredients (except those needed for whipped cream) thoroughly. Grease 2 round deep dish baking dishes and bake at 325° for 2 – 2 ½ hours until pudding turns dark. Mix all ingredients for whipped cream in a chilled metal bowl. Beat until soft peaks form. Serve pudding warm topped with homemade whipped cream. This freezes well, and it makes two. Each dish serves about 8-10.

SOUR CREAM POUND CAKE

I never had the pleasure of meeting my wife's grandmother, but apparently she was a phenomenal cook. Luckily, I have had the pleasure of tasting some of her recipes.

- **2 sticks butter, softened**
- **3 cups sugar**
- **1 cup sour cream**
- **½ tsp baking soda**
- **3 cups cake flour**
- **6 eggs, beaten**
- **1 tsp vanilla**

Preheat oven to 325°F. In a mixing bowl, cream butter and sugar together. Add sour cream and blend well. Sift the baking soda and flour together, and gradually add to the creamed butter alternating with adding the beaten egg mixture. Add the vanilla and pour into a greased and floured 10-inch tube pan. Bake for 1 hour and 20 minutes until an inserted toothpick comes out clean. Will be brown and crusty on top. Let cool before slicing.

KENTUCKY DERBY PIE

When we lived in Augusta, Georgia, my wife and I belonged to a supper club with five other couples. Each couple was assigned a dish, and we met every other month. Once when it was held at our house, we were all featured in a local magazine, and we had to provide all the recipes for print. It became an issue with our neighbor because this recipe was a family secret. In fact, it was so secret, the recipe had not actually been handed down to our neighbor – she had copied it while her mother-in-law was in the shower! It was worth it, though...and it was included in that magazine spread.

- **1 cup sugar**
- **½ cup all-purpose flour**
- **2 eggs**
- **½ cup butter, melted**
- **1 cup pecans, chopped**
- **6 oz semi-sweet chocolate chips**
- **1 tsp vanilla**
- **1 unbaked 9-inch pastry shell**

Preheat oven to 325°. Combine sugar and flour. Add eggs and butter, mix well. Stir in nuts, chips and vanilla. Mix thoroughly. Pour into crust and bake 40-45 minutes. You might need to cover the pie with aluminum foil towards the end to prevent the pie from burning.

Bill West

BACON CHOCOLATE CHIP COOKIES

Several years ago, when we first started doing weekly podcasts, someone sent us some bacon cookies to try. We were excited to try them on the show, and as the saying goes, "Everything is better with bacon!" Here is our version of this truly delicious and unique cookie.

- **5 strips bacon**
- **1 cup all-purpose flour**
- **½ tsp baking soda**
- **½ tsp salt**
- **1 stick unsalted butter (room temp)**
- **½ cup sugar**
- **1/3 cup light brown sugar**
- **1 egg**
- **1 tsp vanilla**
- **⅔ cups semisweet chocolate chips**
- **½ cup chopped pecans**

Place bacon in a large skillet and cook over medium heat 6-8 minutes, turning several times until done. Drain, chop and set bacon aside. Preheat oven to 350°. Line two baking sheets with parchment paper.

Whisk together flour, baking soda, and salt. In a large bowl, beat butter and both sugars. Add egg and vanilla, and beat until blended. Gradually add in the dry ingredients; beat until well incorporated. Stir in chocolate chips, pecans, and chopped bacon. Drop well-rounded tablespoonfuls at least 2 inches apart to allow for spreading. Bake for 10 - 12 minutes until golden brown around the edges. Transfer to a rack to cool. May be served warm, but should be kept refrigerated after they cool. Makes about 18 cookies

WORLD'S EASIEST DUTCH OVEN PINEAPPLE CAKE

Several years ago, we made a video of this one, and I had to hang upside down all day for the shoot...not my favorite memory, but the cake was delicious!

- **7 pineapple slices**
- **7 marischino cherries**
- **1 stick butter**
- **2 cups brown sugar**
- **(2) 1 ½ quart tubs vanilla ice cream, softened**
- **(1) 2-lb bag self rising flour**

Coat a cast iron dutch oven with butter spray and a coat of flour. Melt butter in the bottom of the pan and stir in the brown sugar. Carefully arrange pineapple slices and marischino cherries around in the melted butter and sugar mixture. In a large bowl, mix both tubs of vanilla ice cream with the bag of self rising flour until well blended. This will mix best if icecream is melted. Pour the batter over the pineapple rings, and cover. Simulate a 350° oven by placing about 10 hot coals under the pot, and approximately 17 on top. Remove the lid after about 20-30 minutes and check doneness with a wooden skewer. Couldn't be any easier, and it makes a tasty grilled dessert.

Bill West

Chapter 9

TOP TIPS and SOME WARNINGS

> "Name me a society that doesn't love barbecue? It doesn't exist. Mankind is barbecue celebration."
>
> – **Ted Nugent**

Chapter 9

TOP 10 TIPS

There are so many tips and tricks to share on BBQ that I created an entire website to keep track. Some tricks are unusual. Some tips are useful to only a small few. But when it comes down to the basics it's often common sense. Here are a few tips worth sharing:

1. Need Help?
   When somebody asks you "Is there something I can do to help?" Say yes. I have a hard time with this (the martyr in me). But one of the greatest "helps" can be a simple request for clean up assistance. There are is a lot of delayed gratification in this deal as barbecue is notoriously grimey.

   "Or if they ask Is there anything we can bring?" Be ready with something. Ideas: chips, condiments, ice, a cooler of beverages. Most guests enjoy contributing so it will not only make THEM feel good it can alleviate a task or item that you don't want to manage or lug

   Tailgating? Think creative: tent / fire extinguisher/ wet naps / booze or ice.

2. Serve it Hot
   Remember McDonald's McDLT? Hot side hot. Cool side cool. Take care with resting process and still serve food hot. Hot food pulls in more senses like smell (not to mention hearing the sizzle). Example:

Nothing's better than hot fresh pizza. Even cheap pizza! That steaming slice on the ride home is as good as it gets. That hot fresh now light at Krispy Kreme gets people's attention at a primal level.

3. Let it Rest
I know. Us guys, we want it now. No one has any patience anymore. But you really need to let your meat rest. Consider it a part of the recipe. Especially the bigger cuts. By refraining from cutting into the meat too soon, you allow the natural juices to reabsorb back into the meat making for a juicier bite. Here are three things you can do while waiting for the meat to rest:

- Drink a beer / serve a drink

- Prep the grill for next time (blast & brush see below)

- Ring one of those cool triangle bells spit and yell "Come 'N Get IITTT!!" At the top of your lungs. This is especially fun for apartment dwellers.

4. Sweet Finish

Hold sweet sauces until the end of your cook. Sugar burns. Consider cutting the sugar (to paraphrase a slogan from JB's Smoke Shack here in South Carolina: Taste the flavor in the meat when the sauce on the side).

5. Back to The Grind
Grind your own fresh whole black pepper corns.

6. Keep a LEVEL head
Set up your grill with heat intensity levels. Those are dials on the grill, not switches. The knob actually has different levels and intensity on purpose! Not just high and off. Lol. Even charcoal grills need to have levels and cool zones. I'm totally guilty of ignoring that tip most days.

7. Put a Lid On It

   Keep it closed! The grill lid that is. Keeping the lid closed is obvious but too often overlooked. You could lose ten minutes per peek. The lid also radiates heat from top down more evenly when it's in place. Remember: If it's thicker than your hand close the lid.

   On gas grills, I'll watch the hole during long boston butt cooks. You keep lid closed but if you have concerns you can use that hole to peek. No flames I hope. You have my permission to take action if you see flames coming out the "butt hole."

8. No Fork

   Do not use that long BBQ fork. You don't want to pierce, puncture, or prick the exterior surface of your sausage or poultry. Use the thing for a tent spike instead. You don't want to drain the flavorful juices if you don't have to. For birds: Inject from INSIDE the cavity.

9. Have a dedicated BBQ fire extinguisher. Most competitions require you to have one at your cook site, and they're not expensive. We keep the best deals updated on our resources page.

10. Shut It Down

    Remember to shut down your fuel source.

    Gas grills: Turn off the gas at the tank. I know. You want to say "No Duh!" But it still happens to me all the time. And you're left with an empty tank.

    One of life's biggest distraction is hot BBQ (remember tip two) it's easy to forget what your doing.

Bill West • 191

A FEW "NEVERS"

Some of these I learned the hard way:

- Never use colored toothpicks for anything you don't want to look like circus polka dots.

- Never leave the grill unattended.

- Never use charcoal grills on a wood deck.

- Never move a lit grill - especially on a trailer. Once you hit 35 miles an hour, you may come to find that a few embers were still hot. That new rush of oxygen and the hot ember popping fireworks display coming from behind your truck, and trailer will be very noticeable after dark. Just sayin'.

- Never use scented trash bags for marinating or storing any food product. That is unless you want your BBQ to share a hint of spring fresh baby powder!

- Never keep windex near your brisket spritz bottle. Long story.

US MEASUREMENT EQUIVALENTS

A pinch/dash	=	1/16 teaspoon
½ teaspoon	=	30 drops
1 teaspoon	=	1/3 tablespoon or 60 drops
3 teaspoons	=	1 tablespoon or ½ fluid ounce
½ tablespoon	=	1 ½ teaspoons
1 tablespoon	=	3 teaspoons or ½ fluid ounce
2 tablespoons	=	⅛ cup or 1 fluid ounce
3 tablespoons	=	1 ½ fluid ounce or 1 jigger
4 tablespoons	=	¼ cup or 2 fluid ounces
5 1/3 tablespoons	=	1/3 cup or 5 tablespoons + 1 teaspoon
8 tablespoons	=	½ cup or 4 fluid ounces
10 ⅔ tablespoons	=	⅔ cup or 10 tablespoons + 2 teaspoons
12 tablespoons	=	¾ cup or 6 fluid ounces
16 tablespoons	=	1 cup or 8 fluid ounces or ½ pint
⅛ cup	=	2 tablespoons or 1 fluid ounce
¼ cup	=	4 tablespoons or 2 fluid ounces
1/3 cup	=	5 tablespoons + 1 teaspoon
3/8 cup	=	¼ cup + 2 tablespoons
½ cup	=	8 tablespoons or 4 fluid ounces or 1 gill
⅔ cup	=	10 tablespoons + 2 teaspoons
5/8 cup	=	½ cup + 2 tablespoons
¾ cup	=	12 tablespoons or 6 fluid ounces
7/8 cup	=	¾ cup + 2 tablespoons
1 cup	=	16 tablespoons or ½ pint or 8 fluid ounces
2 cups	=	1 pint or 16 fluid ounces
1 pint	=	2 cups or 16 fluid ounces
1 quart	=	2 pints or 4 cups or 32 fluid ounces
1 gallon	=	4 quarts or 8 pints or 16 cups or 128 fluid ounces

Liquid / Dry Measure equivalents:

1 TABLESPOON =
= 3 teaspoons
= 1/2 fluid ounce
= 15 milliliters

1/4 CUP =
= 4 tablespoons
= 2 ounces
= 12 teaspoons
= 60 milliliters

1 PINT =
= 16 ounces
= 480 milliliters
= 2 cups

1 GALLON =
= 4 quarts
= 8 pints
= 16 cups
= 3.8 liters

1 CUP =
= 240 milliliters
= 8 ounces

1 QUART =
= 2 pints
= 4 cups
= 32 ounces
= .95 liters

Resources

Many of the documents in this book are available as free downloads in high resolution on our website

https://BarbecueTricks.com

http://barbecuetricks.com/**book-resources**

Find the latest downloads versions at

https://BarbecueTricks.com/BluePrint

If there are updated versions of this book
we will notify you if you join our community at

https://barbecuetricks.com/free-newsletter

Much of the material in this book has been produced in instructional video form. Subscribe to the YouTube Channel at

https://www.youtube.com/user/BarbecueTricks

Facebook - https://www.facebook.com/BarbecueTricks

One Last Thing...

I don't want you to head off into the wild world of BBQ without me saying one more "Thank You" for buying this book. I know there are a lot of cook books out there on grilling, and you took a chance on this one.

I hope you also take advantage of picking up my Barbecue Sides and Sauces book for FREE as my gift to you. Get it here: http://barbecuetricks.com/free-newsletter/

Finally, if you liked what you've read, then I need your help. Please take a moment to leave a review for this book on Amazon. I'll read them all, and it will not only help me know what you like but it also really helps spread the word on Amazon. Even a very short note is very appreciated.

Made in the USA
Coppell, TX
12 April 2022